HIGH SHELF

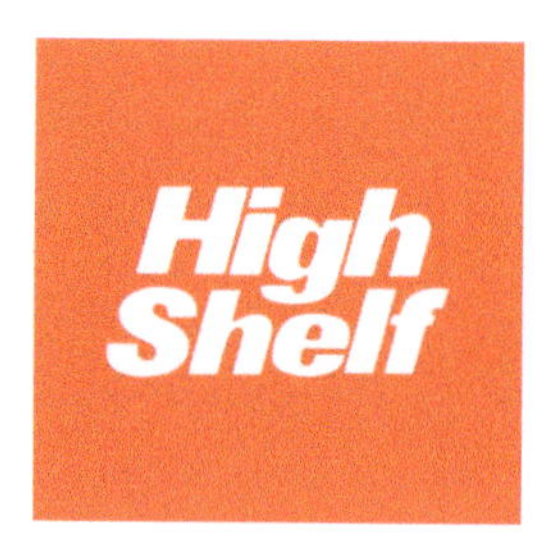

***High Shelf* Issue VIII 5.11.19**

Portland, Oregon.

ISBN:

Cover Image by Monica Wiesblott
Design and Layout by C. M. Tollefson
Edited by David Seung & C. M. Tollefson

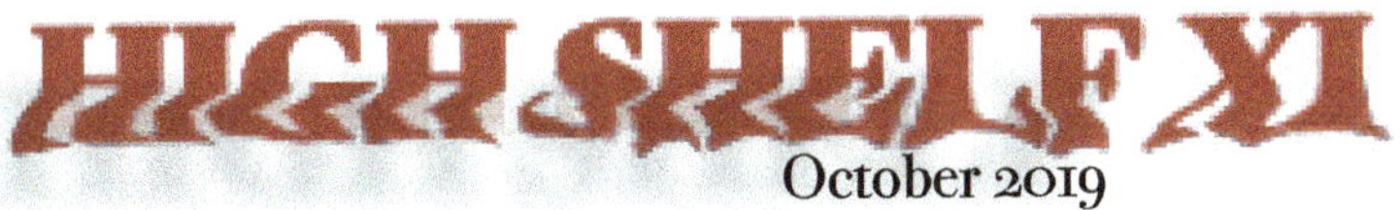

October 2019

"... my fork tongue finally/ empty/ for once/ bless
this bird-chirping silence/ bless/ this breathing hush/... "

Nadine Klassen

"...Through a small space
in the covers, we could glimpse
each other's fate..."

Mollie O'Leary

Table Of Contents

Light Plays on Plants

Collin Randle

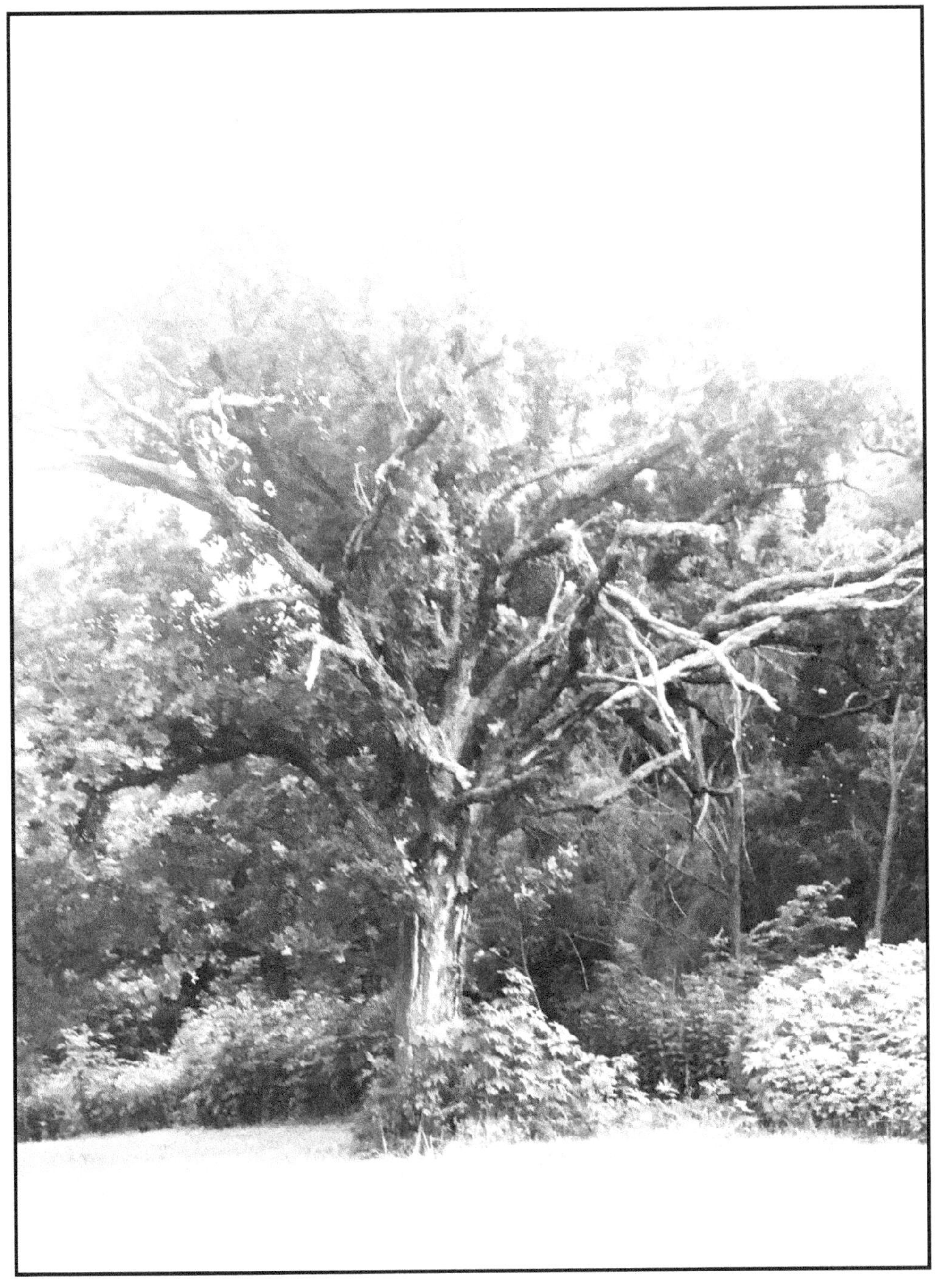

We Were Lying

Alexandra Hubbell

And it was too sweet
With color and light and sound like
coins hitting pavement.

A book studied under its sister trees
Did they see death before them?
Did they want to cry out?
Slices, pages, stained with words fading fast, too fast,
Read by our clawed, gentle hands.
We all searched for meaning before the dawn.
We tried to make it between
sheets of paper and cotton.

Who's saving us now?
Among the metal and the cinder
You were beautiful and sharp and free.
Notes made tones that resonated
from the smallest tips of the tallest pines,
And I saw His face in the leaves
and it blurred around me.

Fountains touched by sinners' hands, soaking their naked bodies,
and stars reflected off the rocks.
Bandanas made with bleach spotted color,
Someone caught us meeting in the corner.

Now, I wonder if age had met you yet
In face and mind and body.
There was no body when I arrived,
All emotion
dripping down and sticking
to the soles of our shoes.
Holding each other, searching for that same meaning,
Books and beds deceived us.
Wherever you are, just remember me in seasons.

We climbed too high to see that you were still underwater.
Temptation took the shape of strings and boards and plastic chairs.
But I remember I envied you
with grains in my braid and
flecks in my eyes and

not the shadows beneath them now.

Hands behind necks and foreheads pressed to glass
There was an act involved in all our scraping and falling.
We tried to draw bridges over flames.
I don't remember your face now, but
as it was. Spinning, and tonguing, and flying.

We were lying.

airplane

Cosper Ashley Emma

the missing is not spread between many, or even two points,
but draped over one like a blanket on a broomhandle,
that is why I'm writing about you

when I think of you, I see for some reason,
a porcelain plate of black olives sitting on the chalky moon

and of your thin, long feet propped up on on the edge of the worn, velvetine couch, pale and casting blue
your legs across my lap,
so when I leaned onto you
they looked enormous against the cold window
pushing back brooklyn in january

eclipsing an airplane that flew through them
like its wings were needles and you and your mythical feet were a totem they pricked into being with opal thread

I know I really love someone when I like the smell of tobacco on them-
but it also reminded me, more constantly than usual
that you will die

I feel bad for the way we fell apart,
but I had to become someone new
before I felt it

exodus hong kong

xiao yue shan

close are those days we stayed past our welcome,
passing around raw peanuts, complaining
about the heat, arms slung around one another's waists
as if mere holding would be enough to starve
the impetus of leaving. in the city that looks too much
like the one we left you continued to look stunned
for a moment after I said, struggling to hold on to
a bag of broken apples, *let's go.* decrepit buildings in
cracking pink shells, lights that closed and opened green
chasing dawn, here, our temporary holding, sitting
around the kettle silver with sweat, glinting against
the skins of midnight roads like oil paintings
left in the shadows. amongst those who ran from
the mainland holding books we compared copies
to determine the multiples, and ripped their pages
to lay between the cotton during winter. we all became
acquainted with the different tastes of hunger—
paired alongside fear it took on the tang of metal,
and with exhaustion the gravity of dust. yet hong kong
remained the reprieve from a home that clotted
bad blood in the center of our bodies, beating
like a second heart that continued its insistence
of running. the sense of never being far enough,
a heart that convinced us in our own beds
that this was just a place to sleep
because it was too late to go home.

Sceneries

Ruben van Gogh

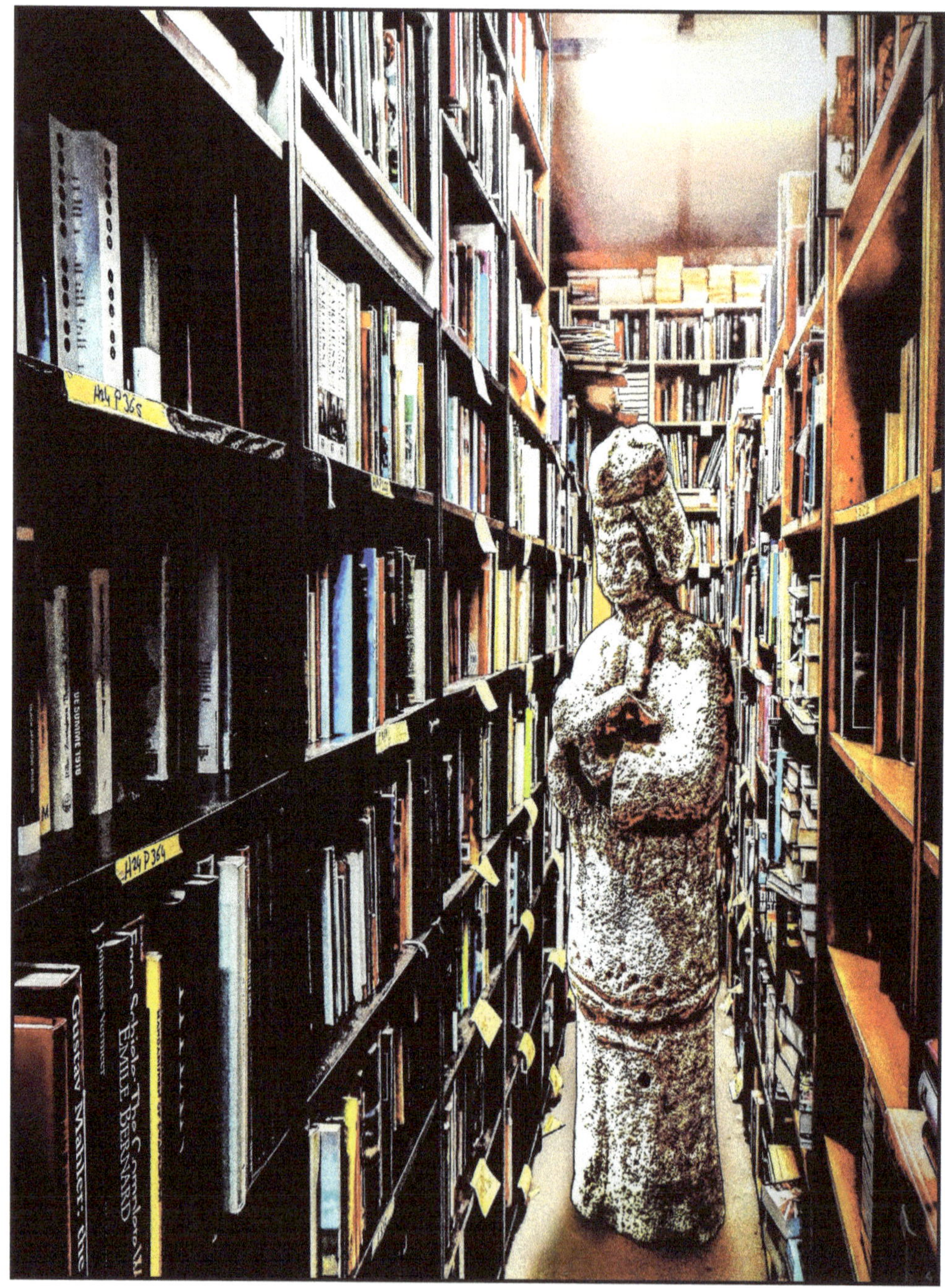

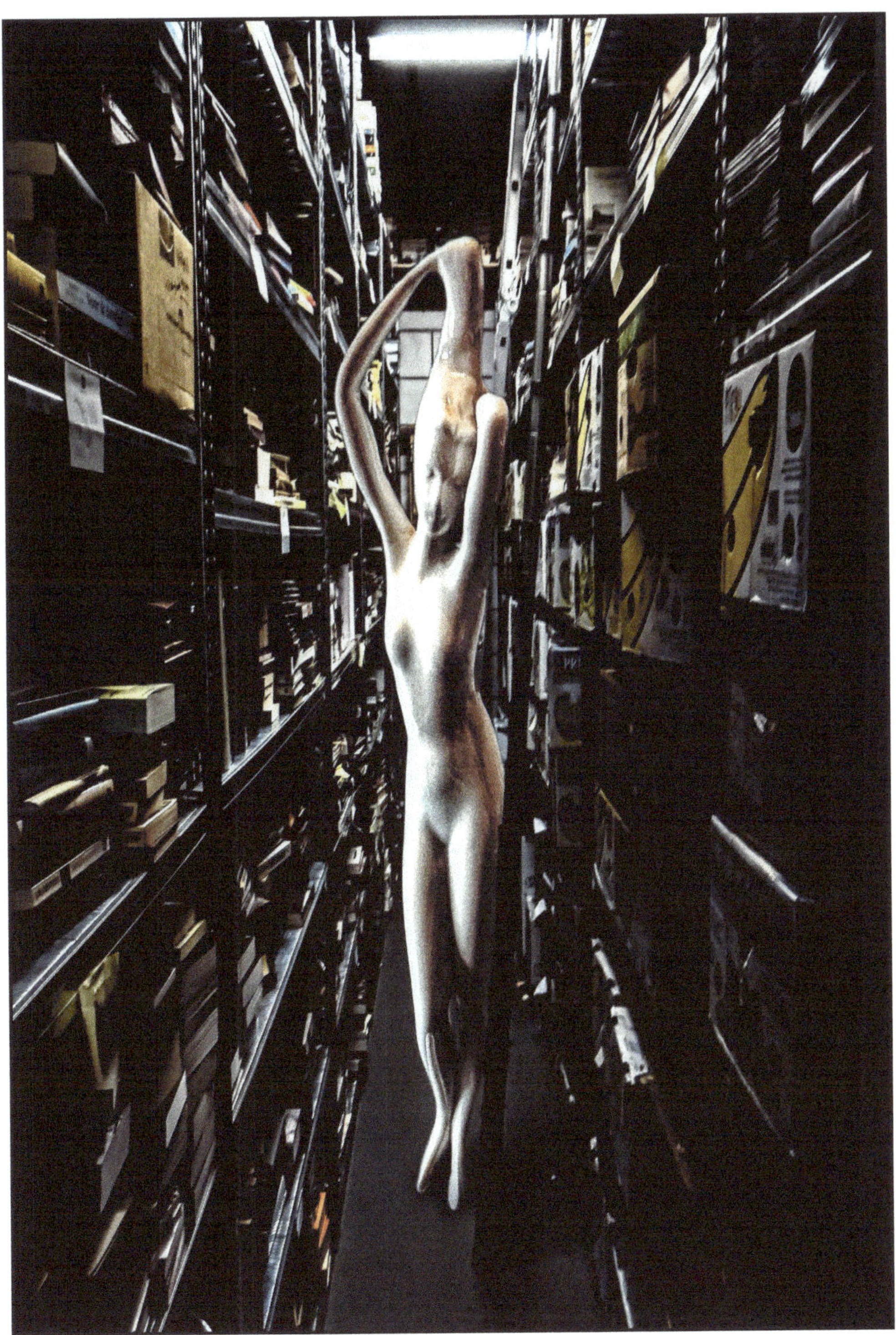

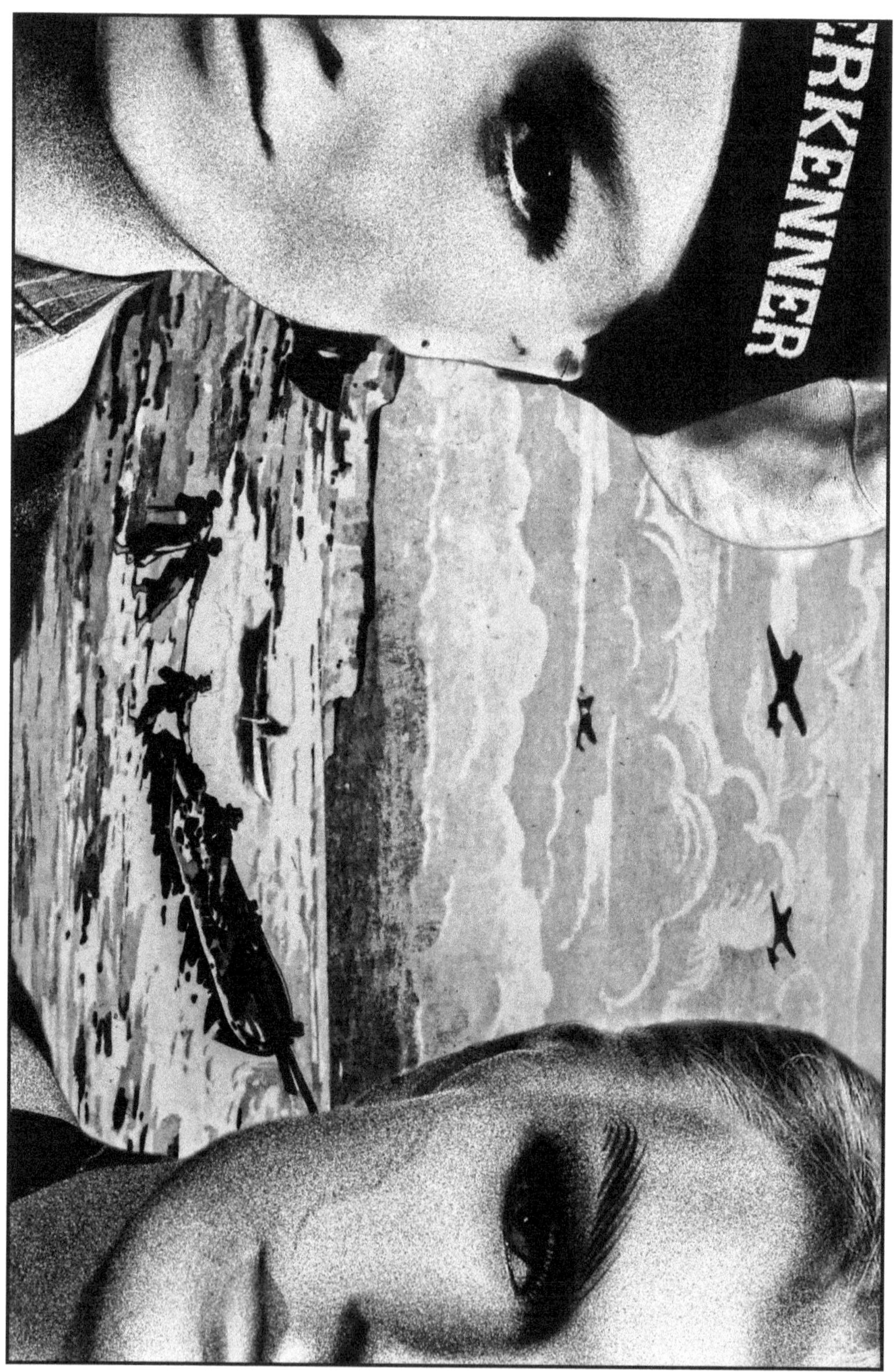

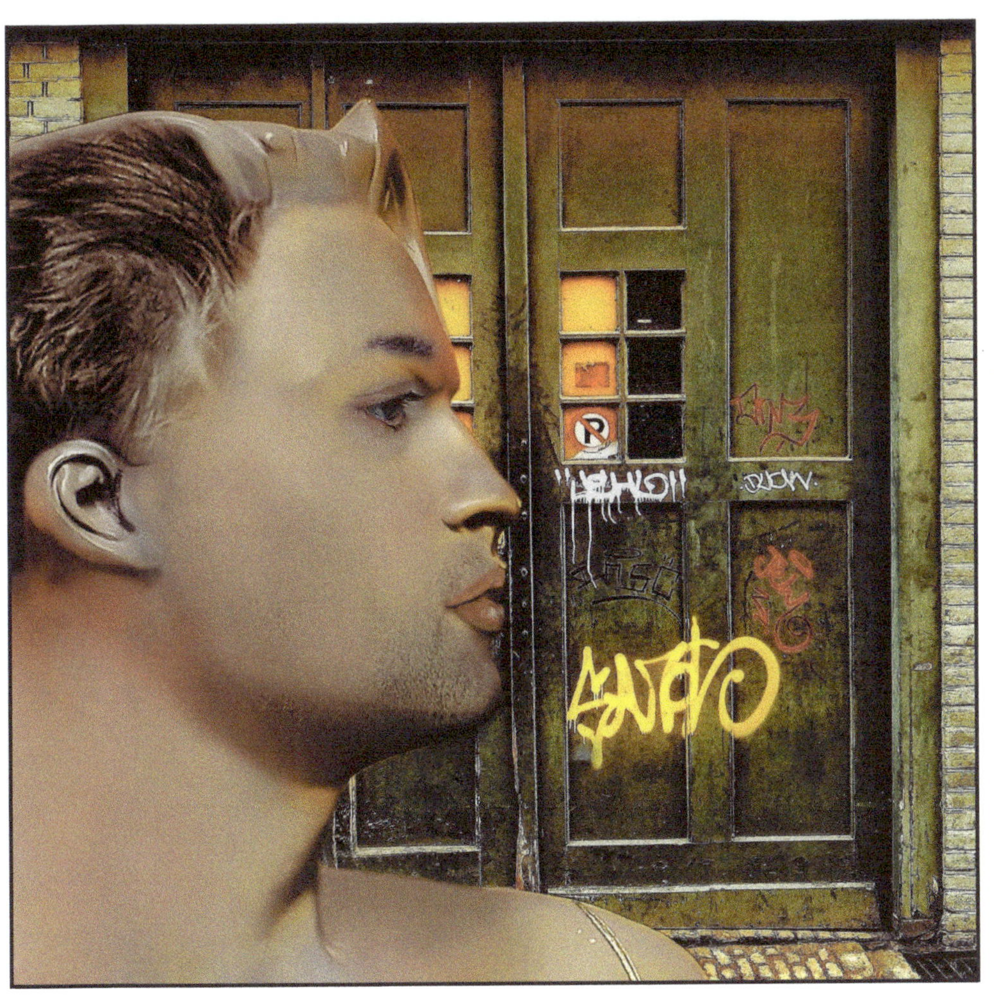

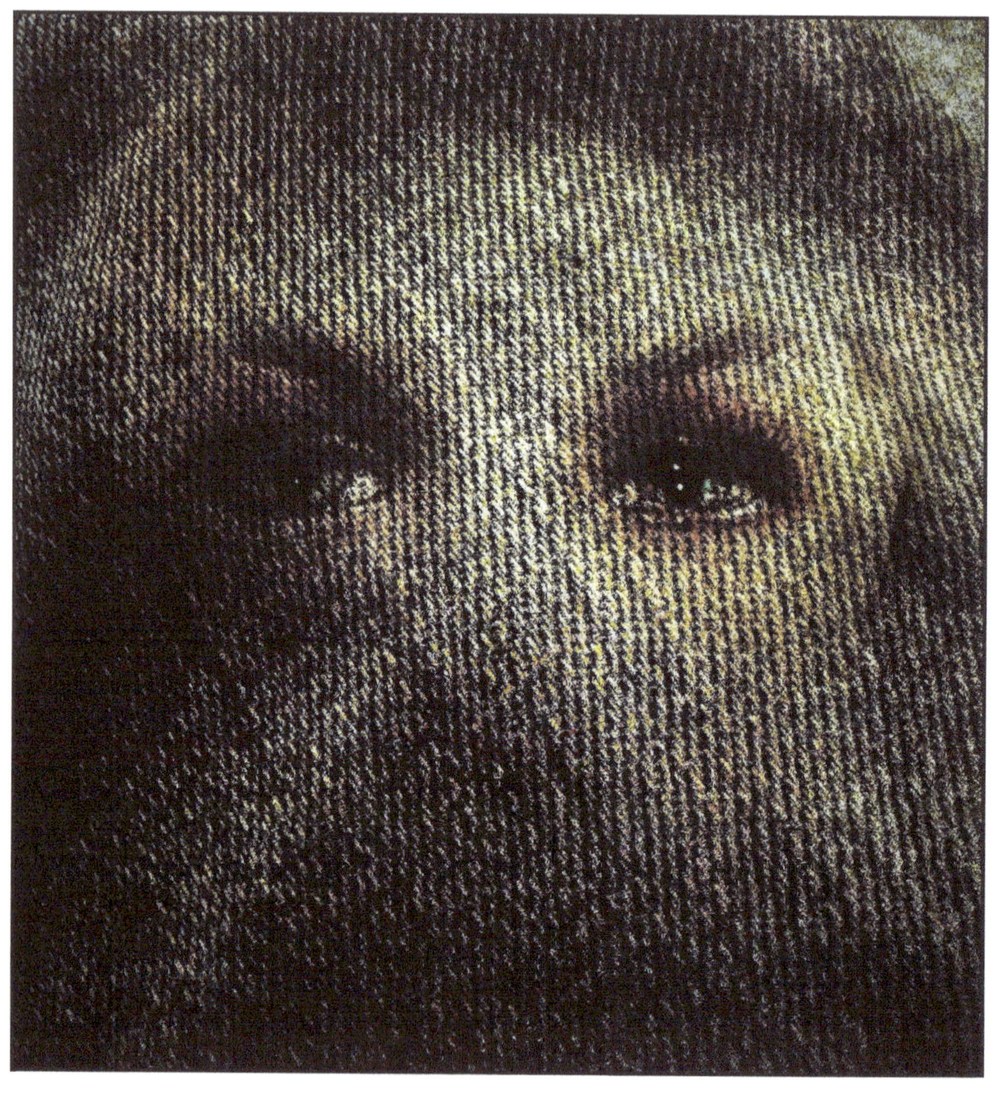

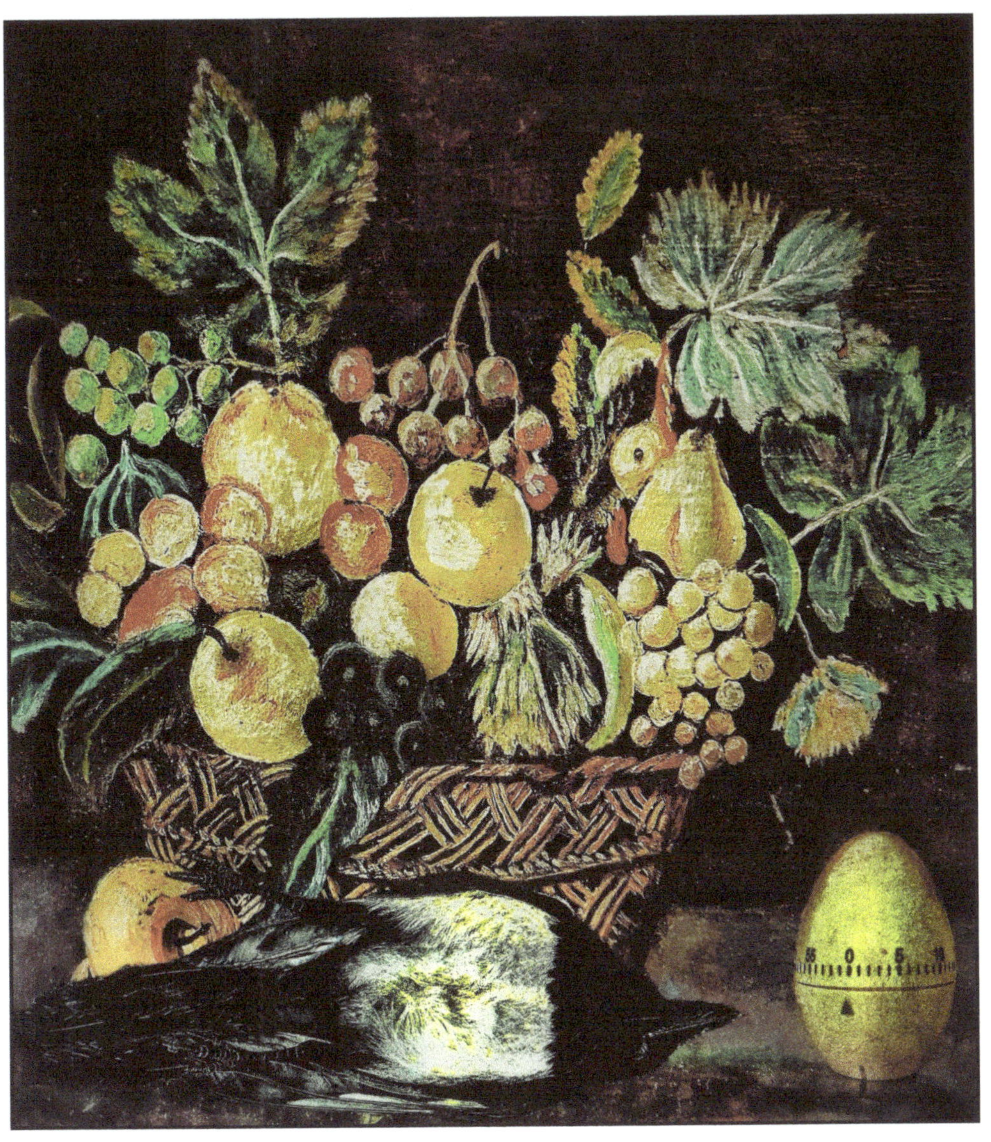
0 5

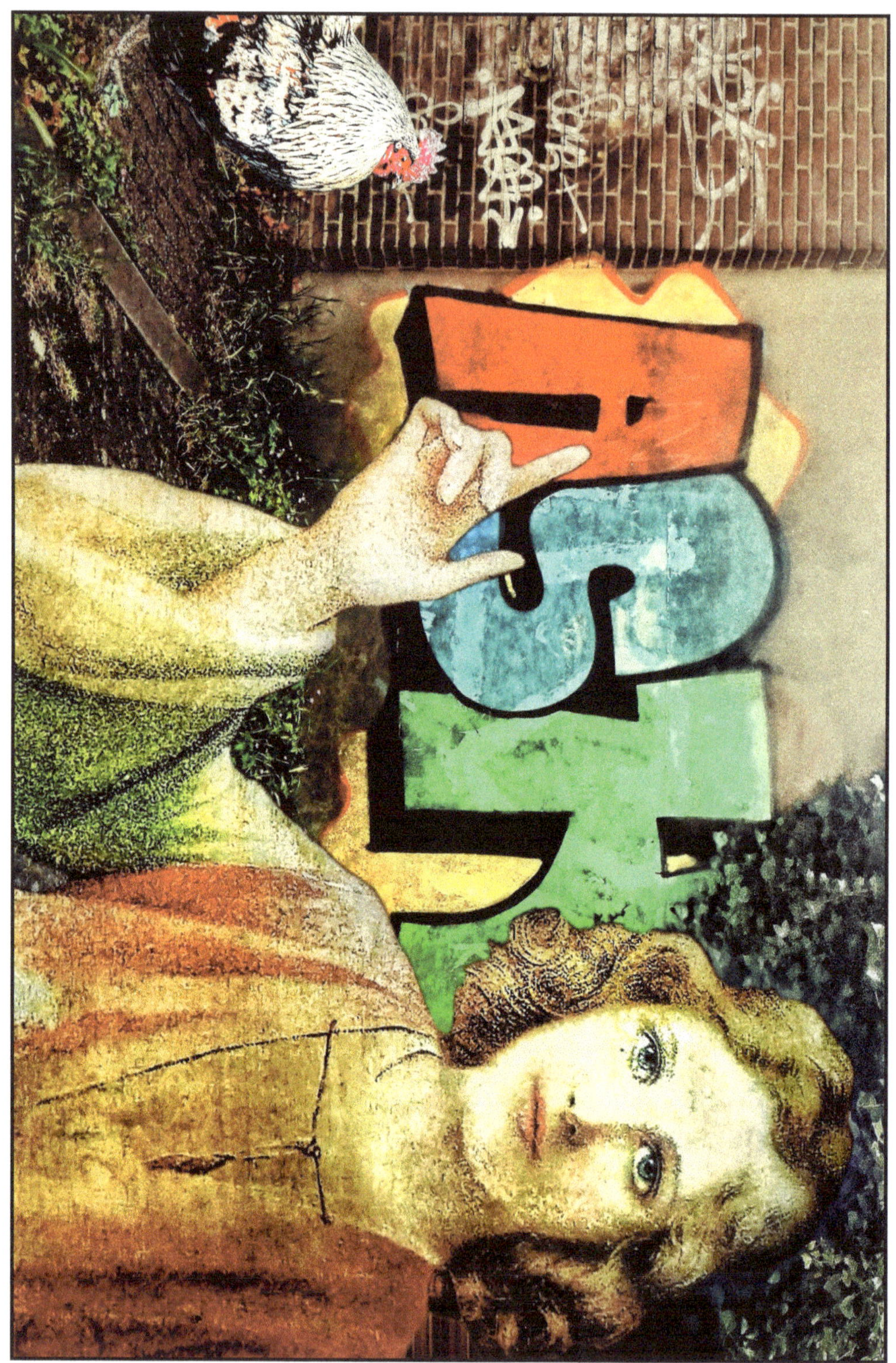
ASL

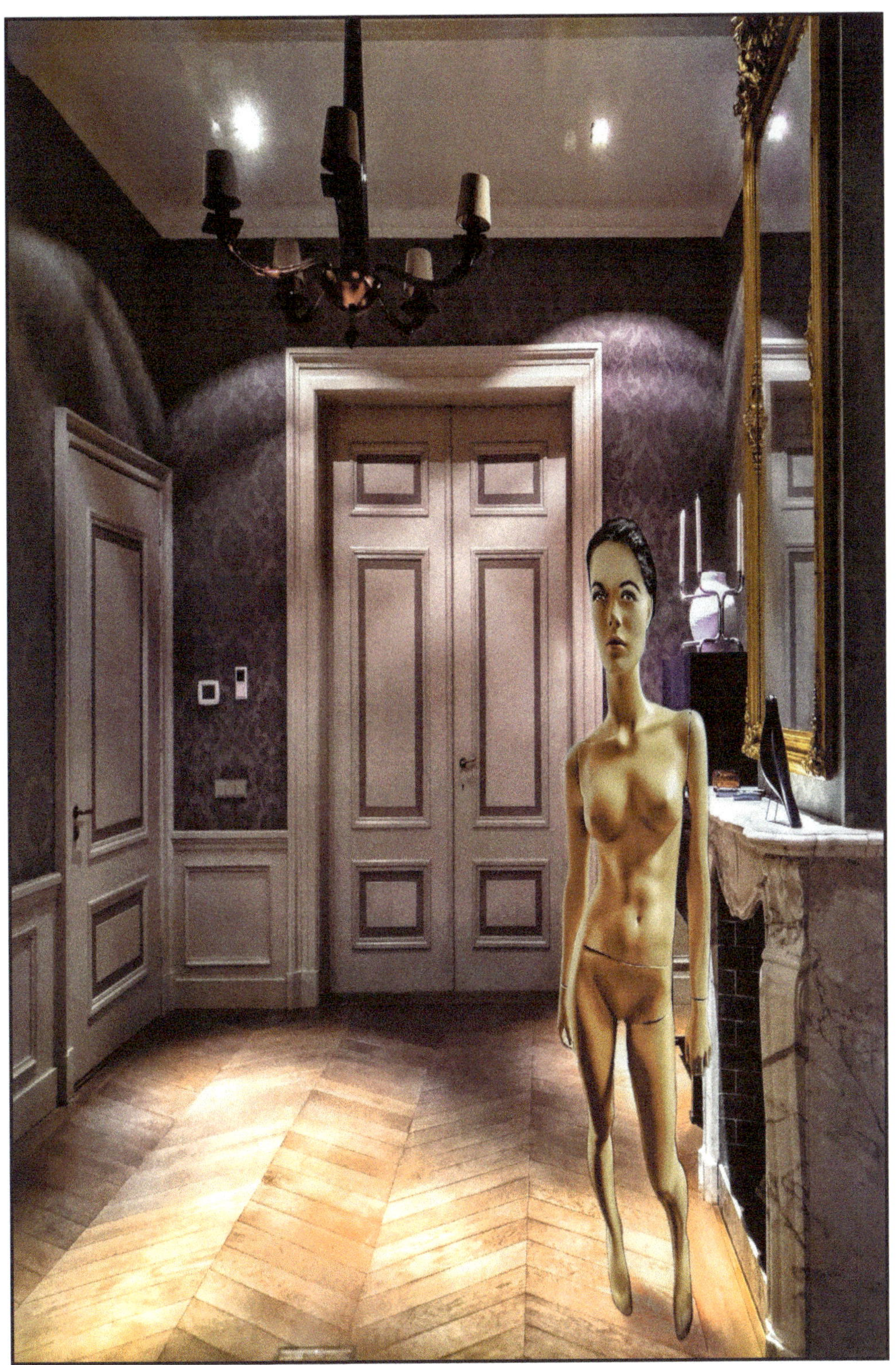

My body's made of shatters.

Juliet Lauren

You ask me if I think humans look foreign as you leave rats heads and dead roses on my doorstep.
Those months where we went crazy with blood flavored religion.
Drumbeats like miles for answers.
The underworld in my brain tissue.
Heavenly angel give me chills like a broken pencil sharpener.
Oh, momma they keep messing with my head.
Oh, momma show me what I should do instead.
Is it my fault or the men's that I'm beautiful in a dirty way?
You are a life and it's fascinating she tells me.
But deep down I know
I'm all and only flat beer and fried nerve endings.
She tells me the blisters and begging will make modern divinity taste sweeter.
That my only god should be my higher self but percentages stain my teeth.
And I belong wherever terrorists and overly sexual babysitters go.
They'll never get their daughter back.
She lost all her innocence when the Beatles started making her sad.
Or maybe when she realized a spoonful of sugar makes cheap wine go down.
Or maybe when she got in the habit of hearing I love you from four different men at the same time. I hate to be the first to admit it but no amount of whiskey is going to help me figure out where we go when we die.
No matter how many spoonfuls of anorexia I slurp I still have no god.
No amount of highs will stop the thoughts from intruding.
No amount of showers I take at a strangers house will get me clean.
I can't help but wonder if I'll corrupt under gray or gold.

My Fork Tongue Finally Empty

Nadine Klassen

the morning is like a cotton-gloved hand/
to my silverware body/ edged/ etched/ with your
initials into my/ spooned spine/ soft/ edged/
milk-white light like/ tiger-stripes through blinds/
my fork tongue finally/ empty/ for once/ bless
this bird-chirping silence/ bless/ this breathing hush/
bless/ these thoughts wearing thin/ thinner/
than the knife they were before/ now/ edged/
in milk-white light

Sunday (on the verge of collapse)

Sophia Lee

splayed newsprint with the comics extracted
(proof of life after last night)
dog food bowl goes untouched
(everyone is afraid to be violent)
footsteps on the stairs
(means we hold our breaths)
squinting and listening
(for a sign, say)
the rustle of pajamas
(on another bare back)
or a divine green light
(dare you to move)

Castles in the Air

Jada Fabrizio

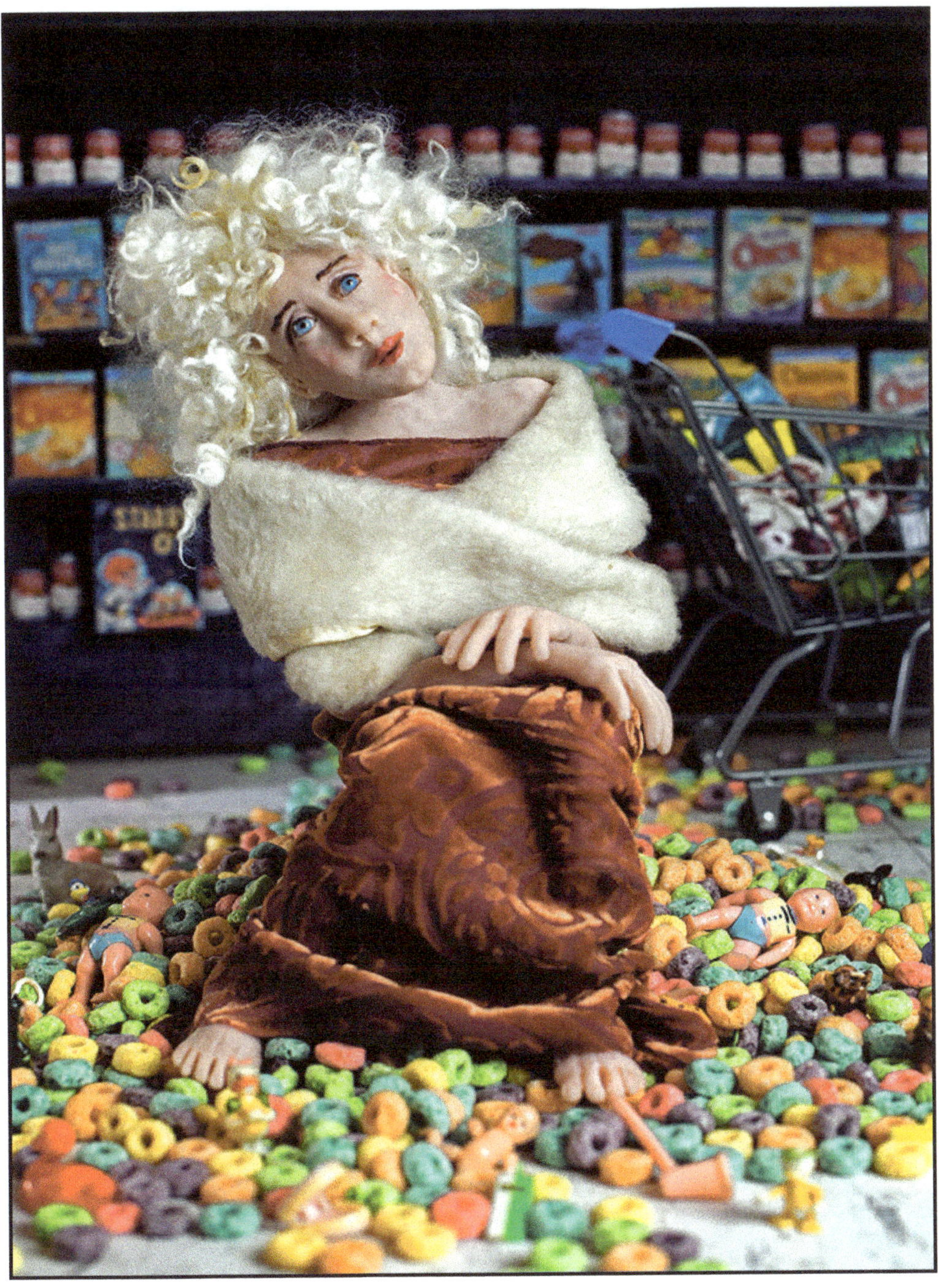

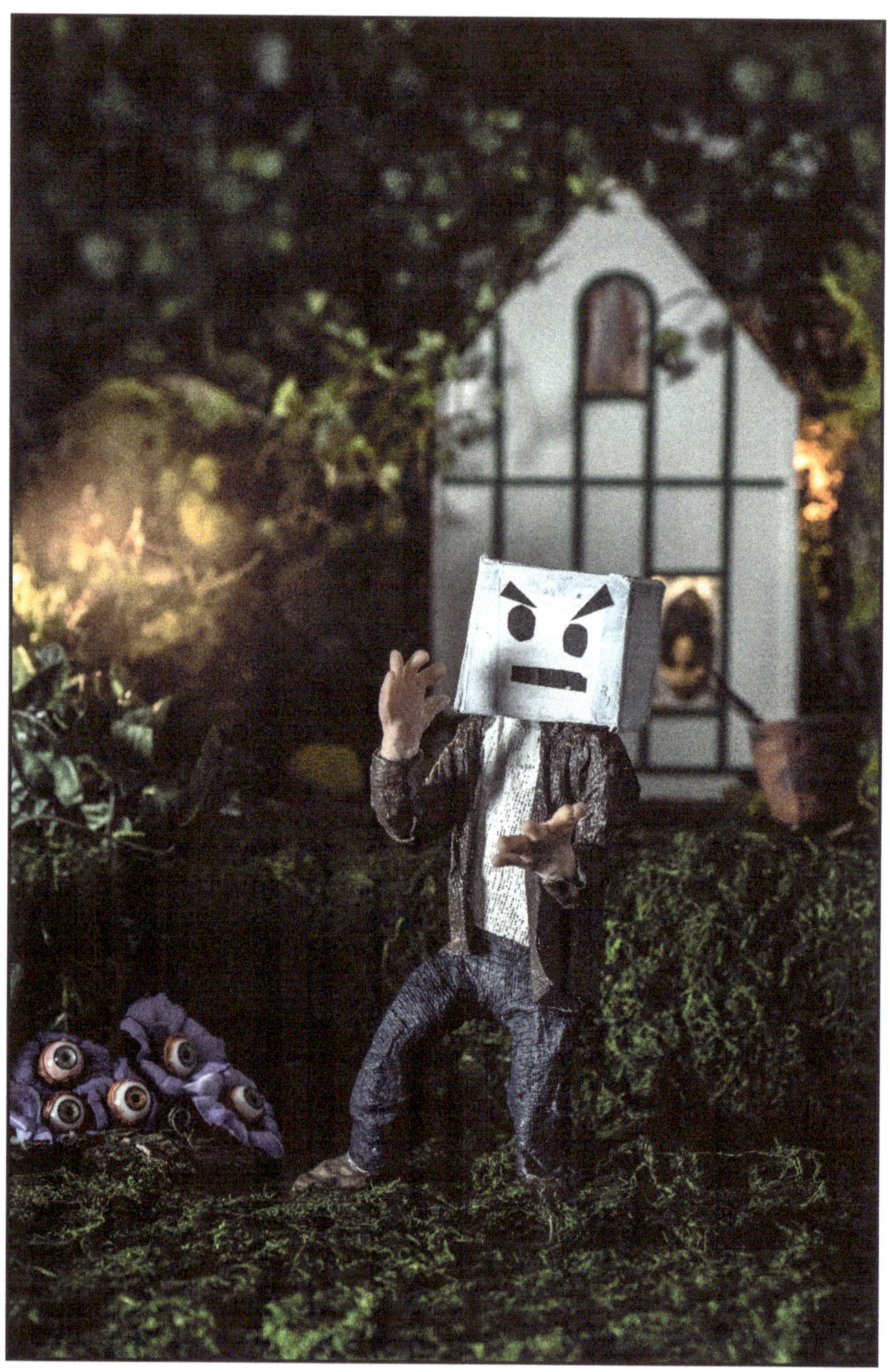

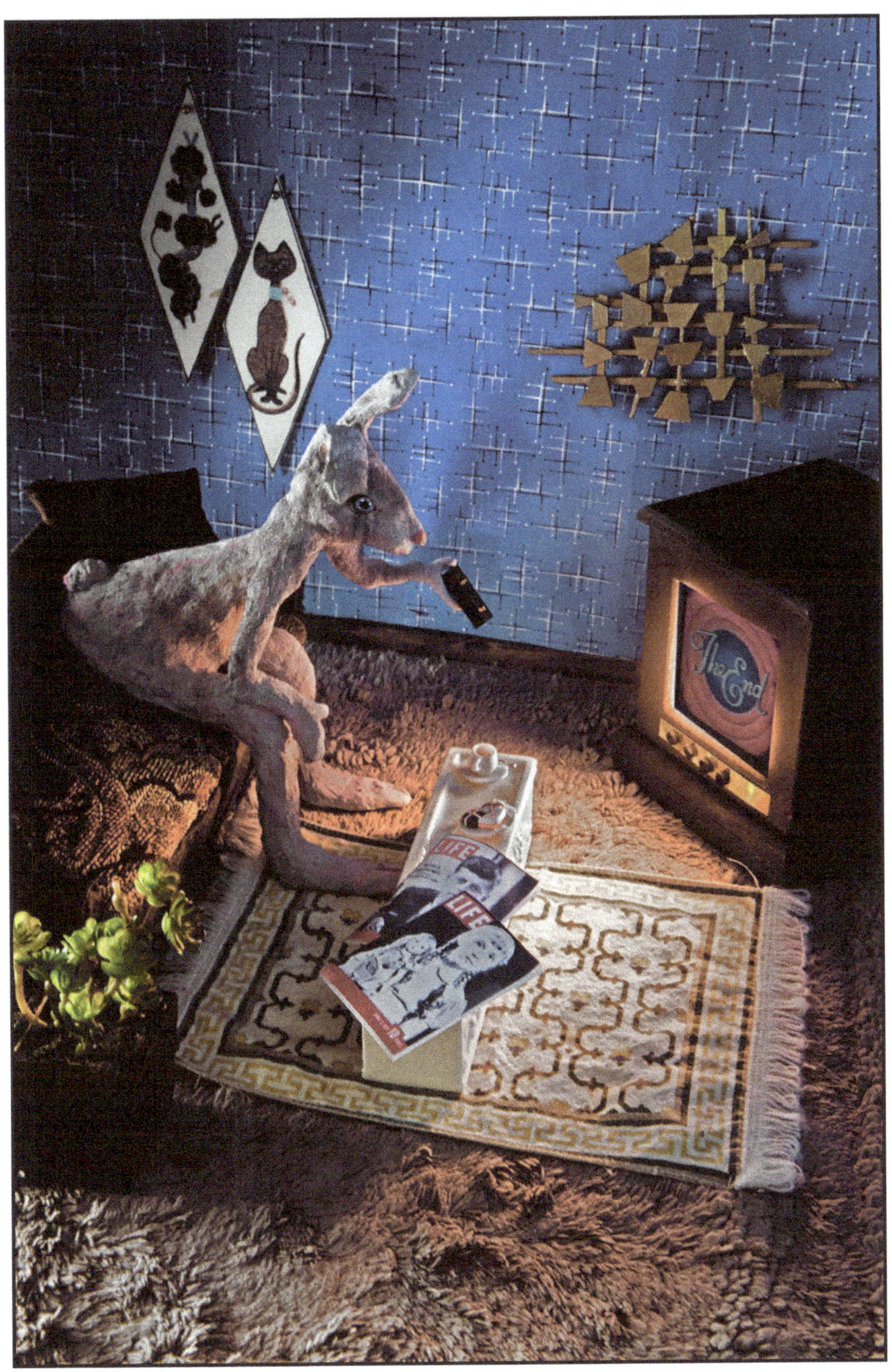
The End
LIFE
LIFE

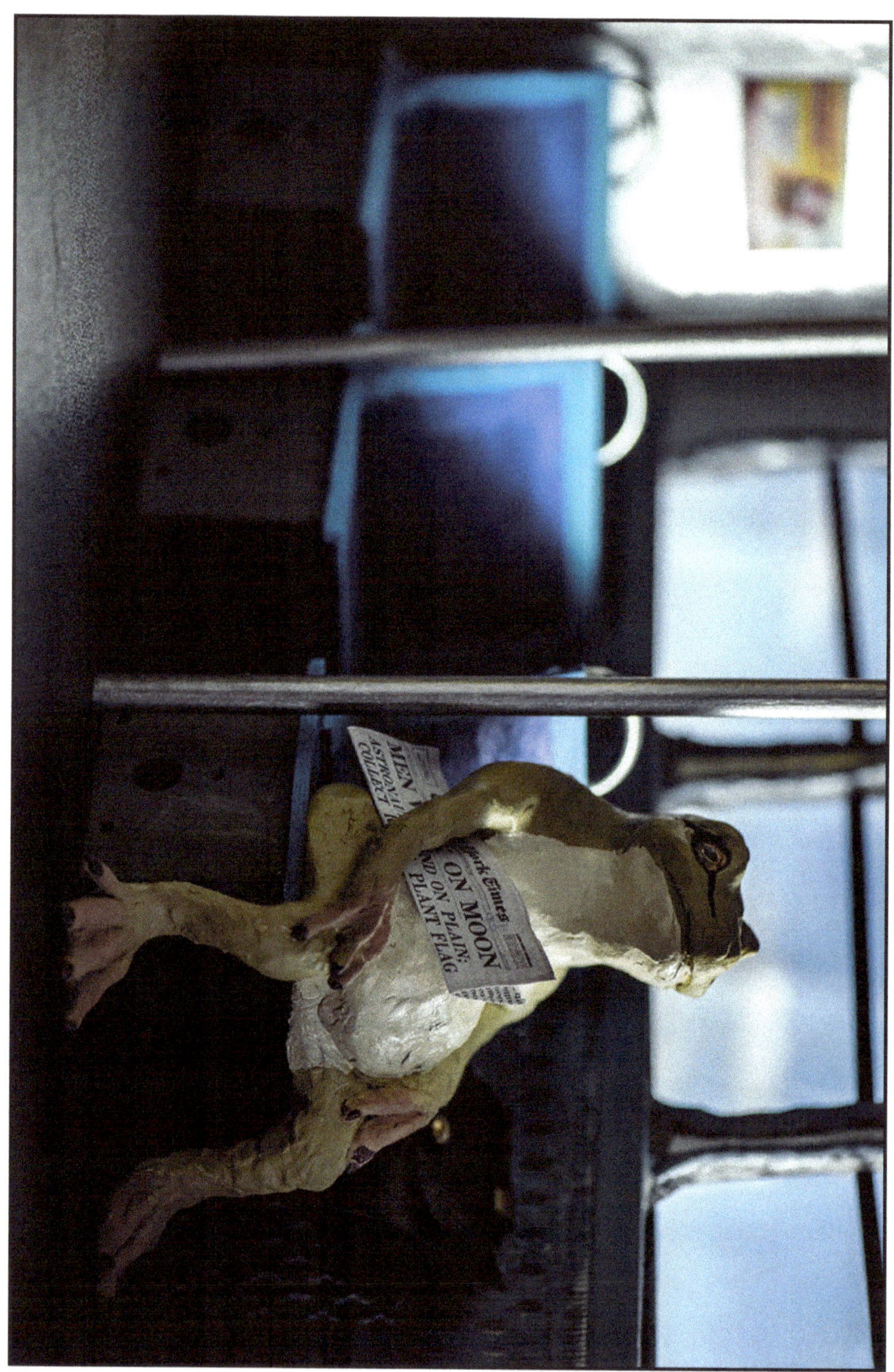
MEN
ON MOON
PLANT FLAG

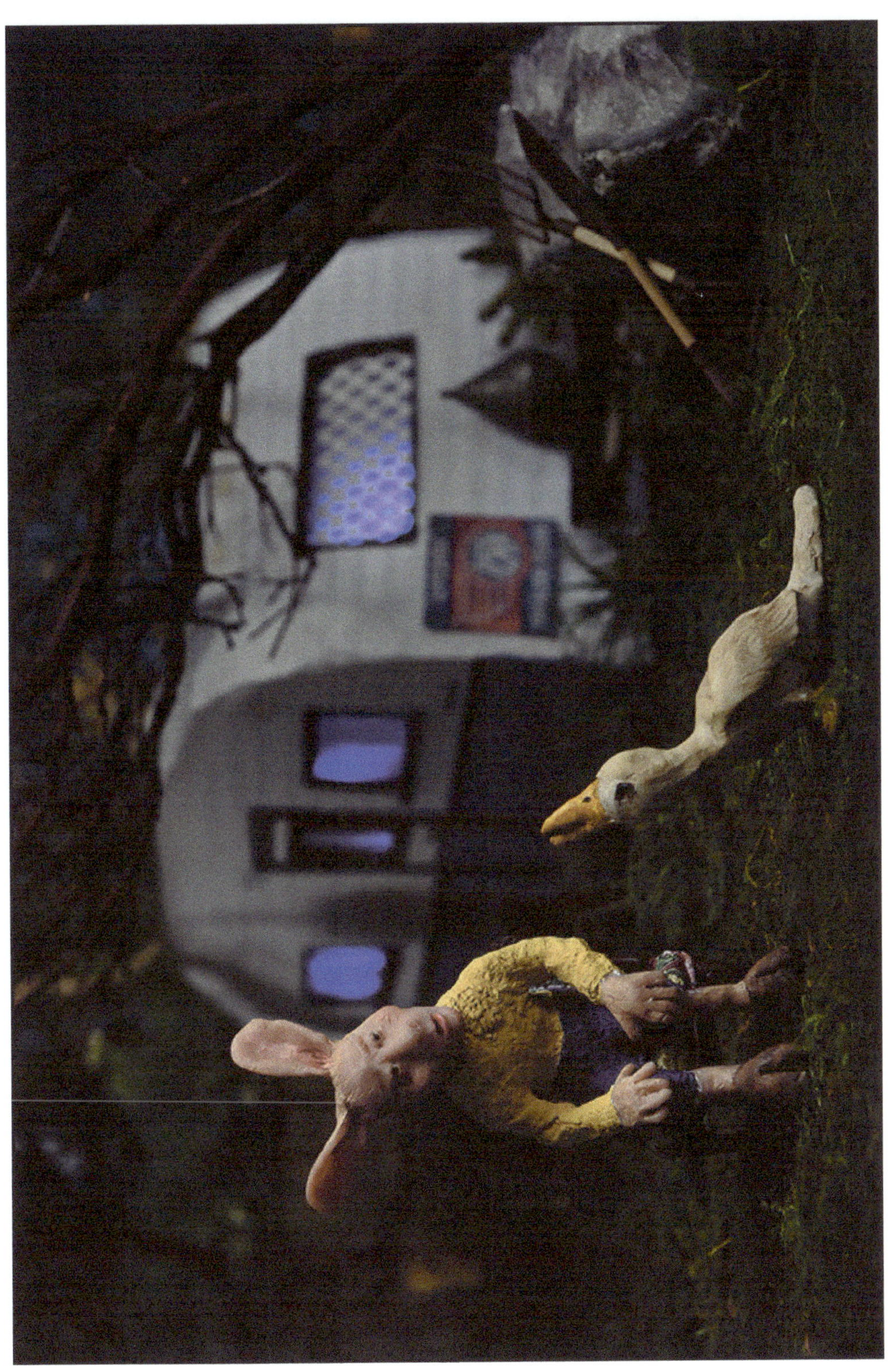

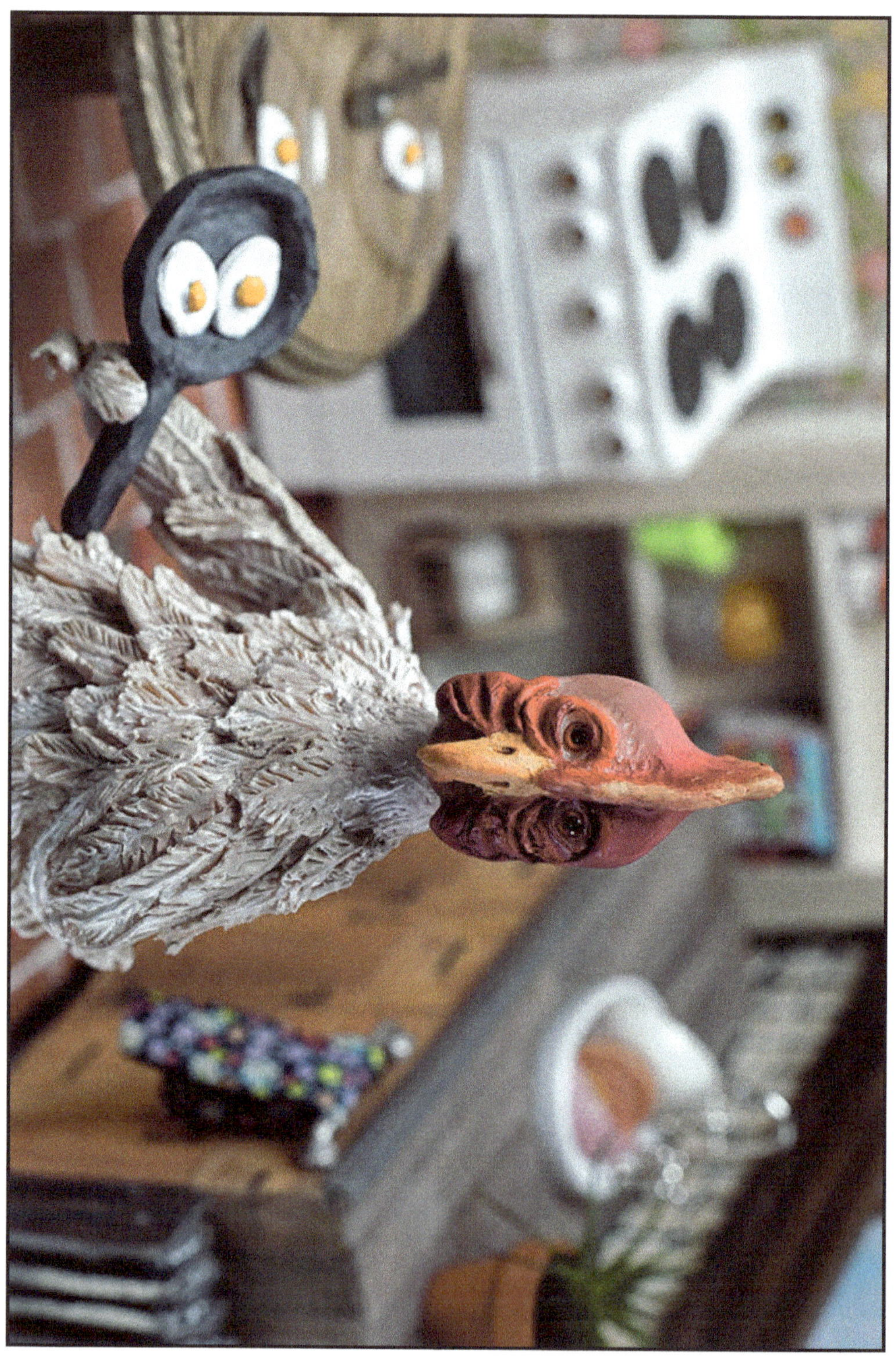

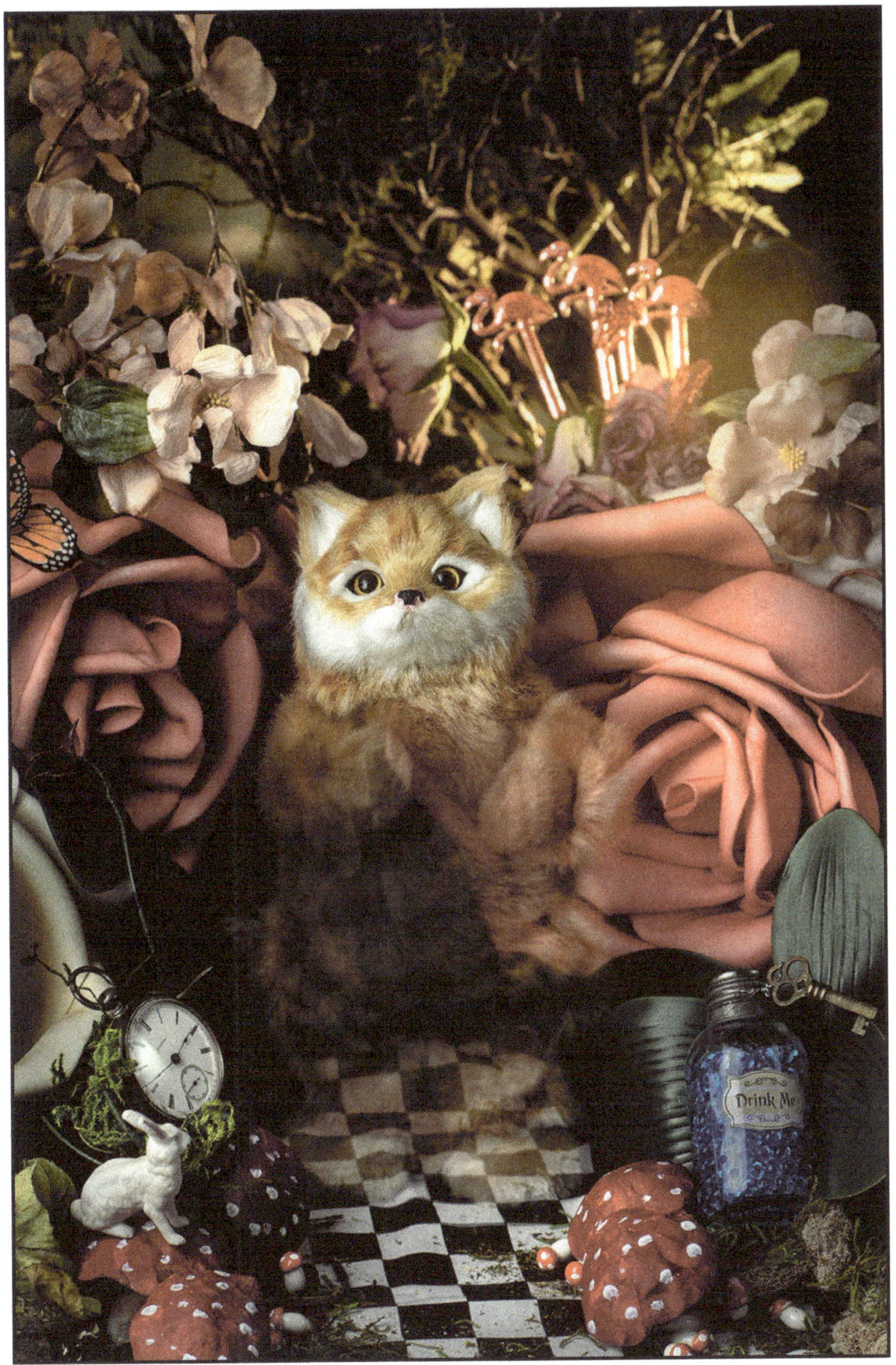
Drink Me

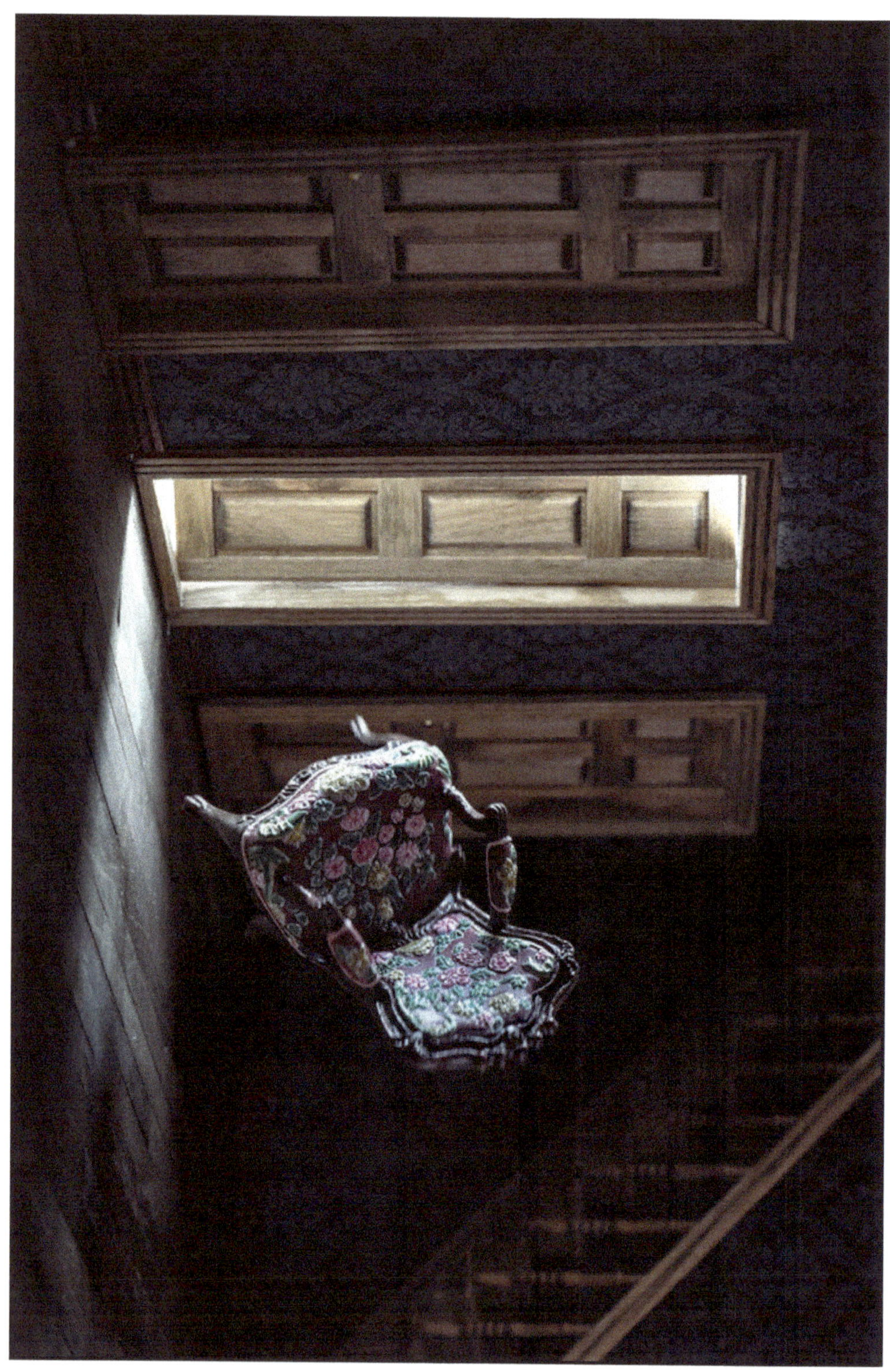

Tongue

Aminta Meheru

The apex moves an identical death
from vellum's firm cradle of fear,

not to do at all against sound but
sound surface for prominent images.

Prominent ideas about neuroimaging
confirm she is only sleeping:

"Detects prey by violent movement
and is not dead at all here in this pond".

But sits there in my dark home,
dreaming around like a gun.

milk bags reserved for human children

Florina Nastase

in the mirror, the handsome rat smirks
and licks his protruding lip, bidding me do the same,
and i oblige, as i bring my head close,
press my cheek against the vanity
so that his little adhesive tongue slips into my ear,
whispering about the babies he hatched inside me,
the nursling rats nestling and nesting between my breasts, gnawing
on the milk bags reserved for human children,
gnawing until they break the bags, and i cry
milk and there are no children
anywhere.
i move my head away from the mirror
and see the rat, still smirking, malevolent, wishing he could outlive me,
watch me grow old,
but every other month he dies. i see him,
deflating like a carnival toy, and a new rat greets me in the morning,
accusing me of trying to make their whole race extinct.
i just don't like being an animal, i tell him,
i don't want to have things grow inside me,
even as they reflect me, even as i'm reflected in them.
i'd like to throw away the bags,
i'd like to let the milk boil over the stove, curl up like smoke.
i'd like that smoke to feed no one.
i'd like to be the mirror, the cold surface between
one rat and the other.

Hidden Sources of Water

Dave Sims

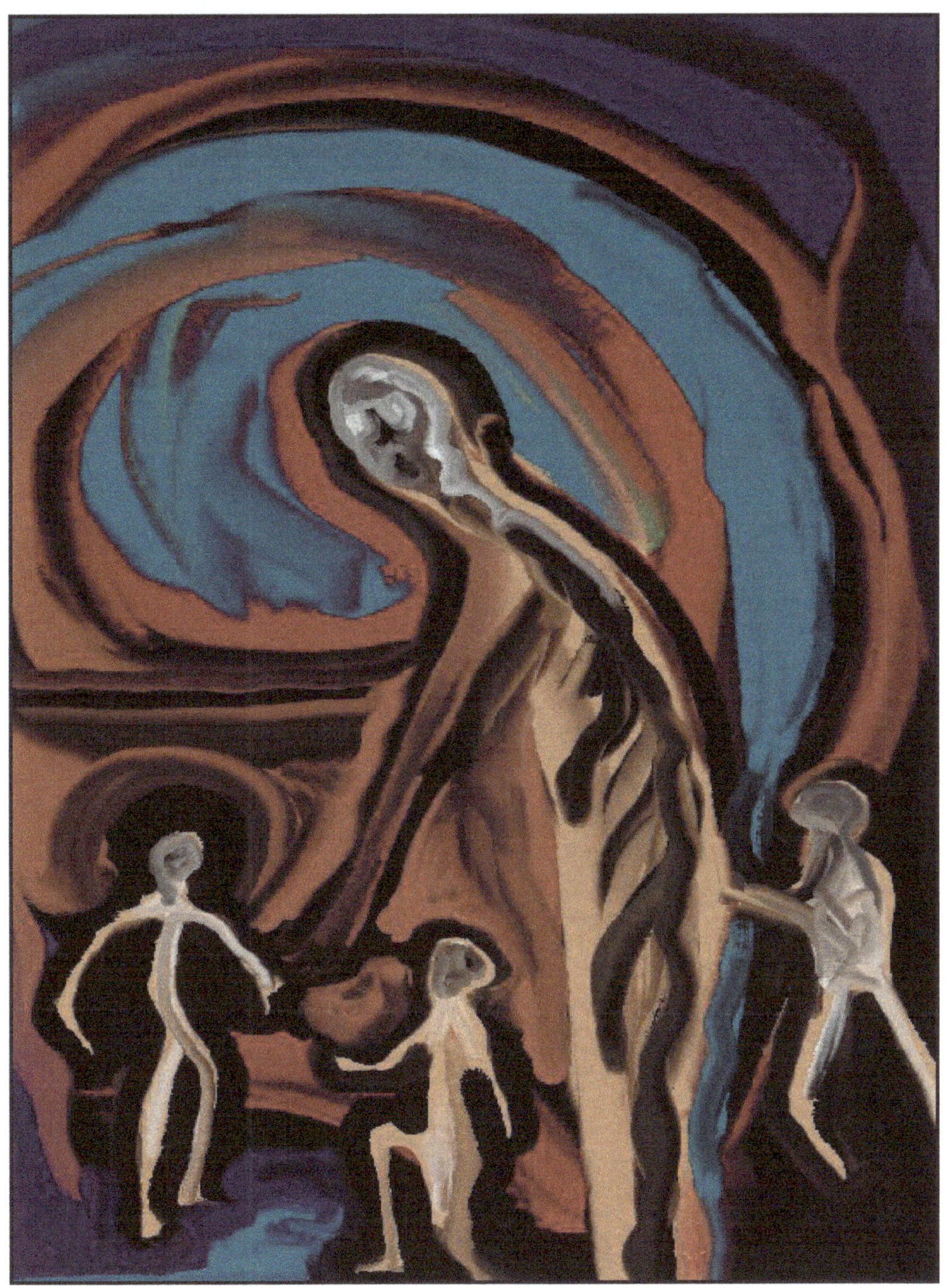

Hidden Sources of Water

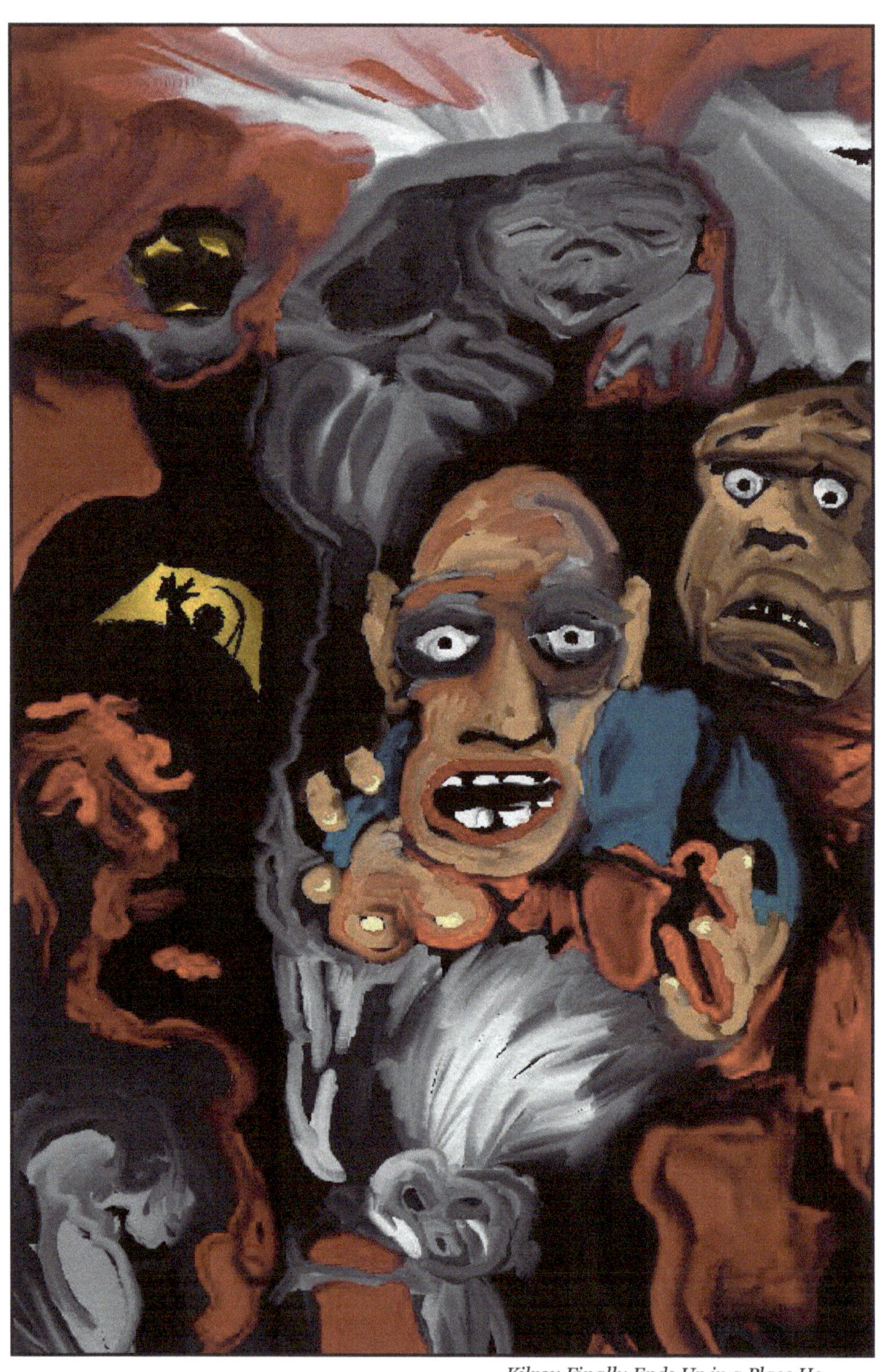

Kilroy Finally Ends Up in a Place He Wishes He Wasn't

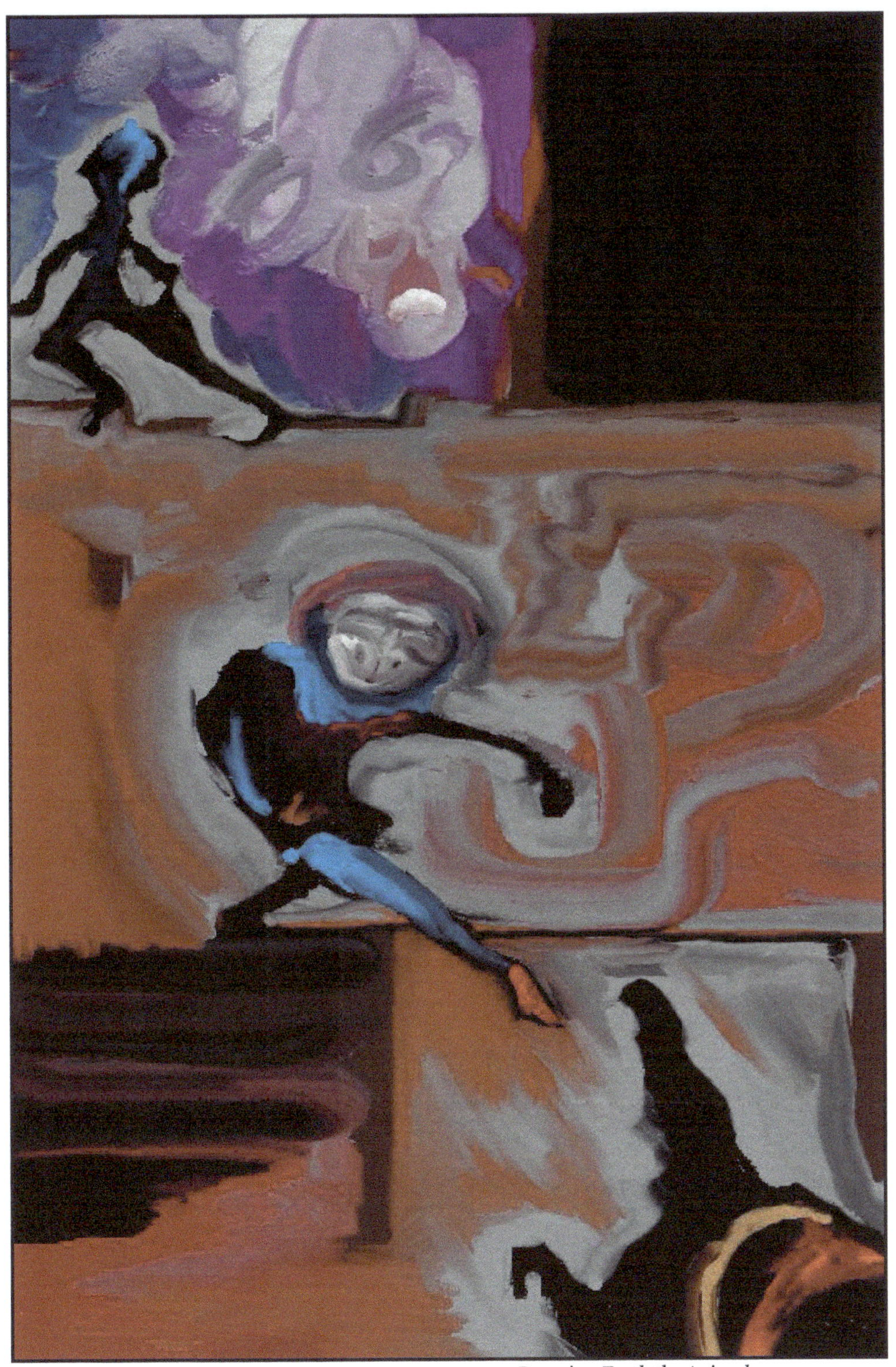

Drawing Forth the Animals

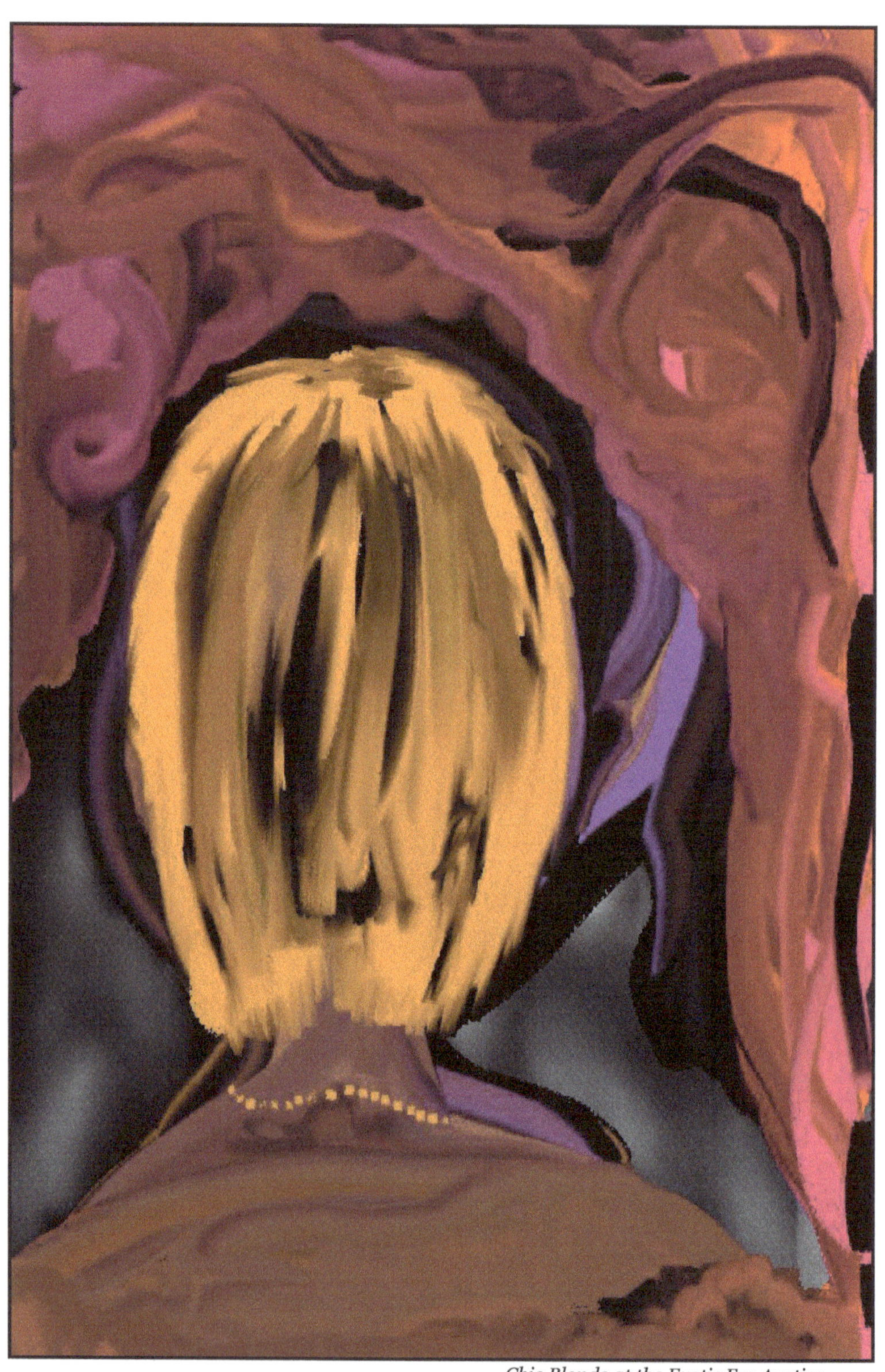

Chic Blonde at the Exotic Fur Auction

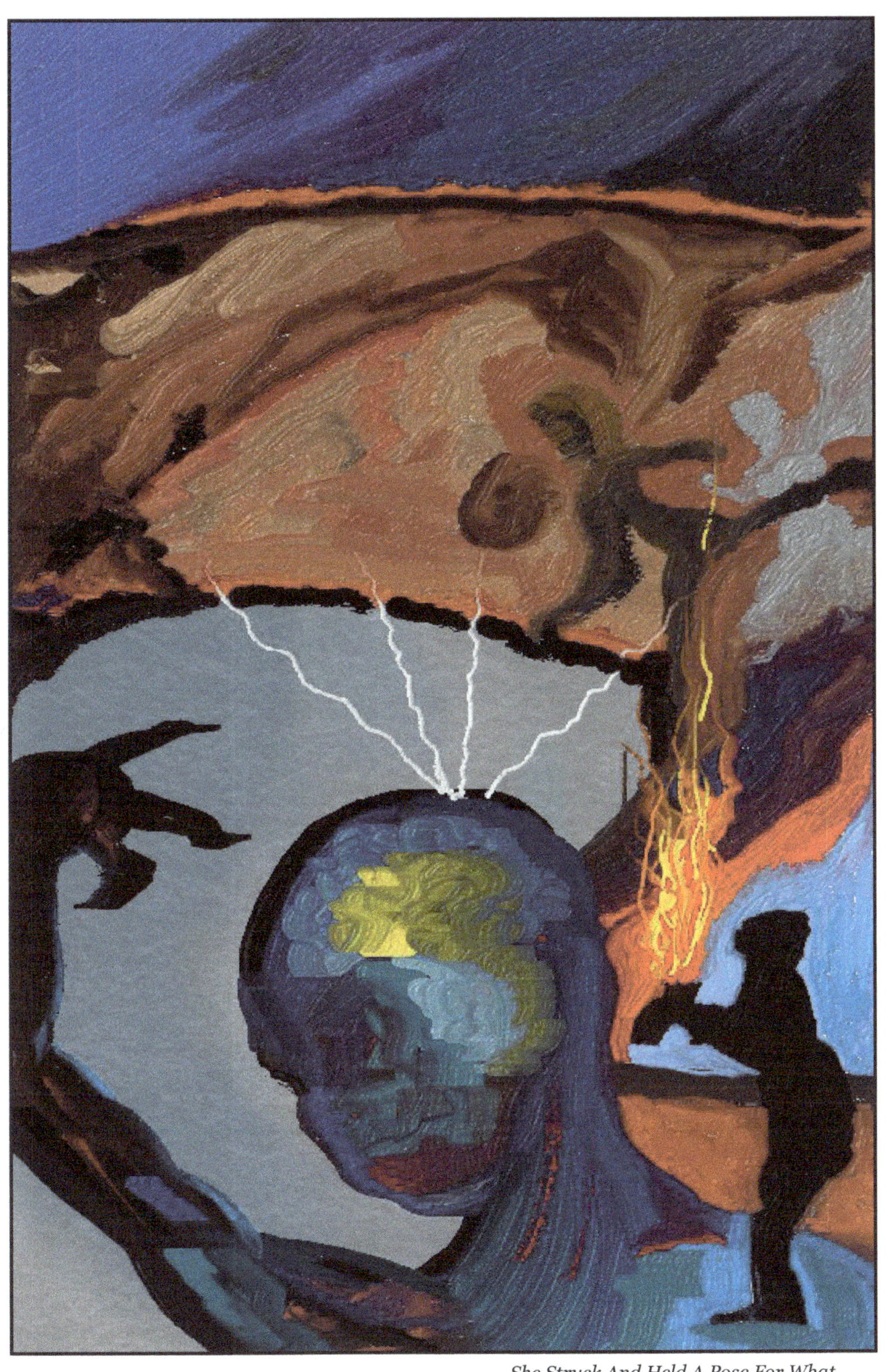

She Struck And Held A Pose For What Seemed Like Forever

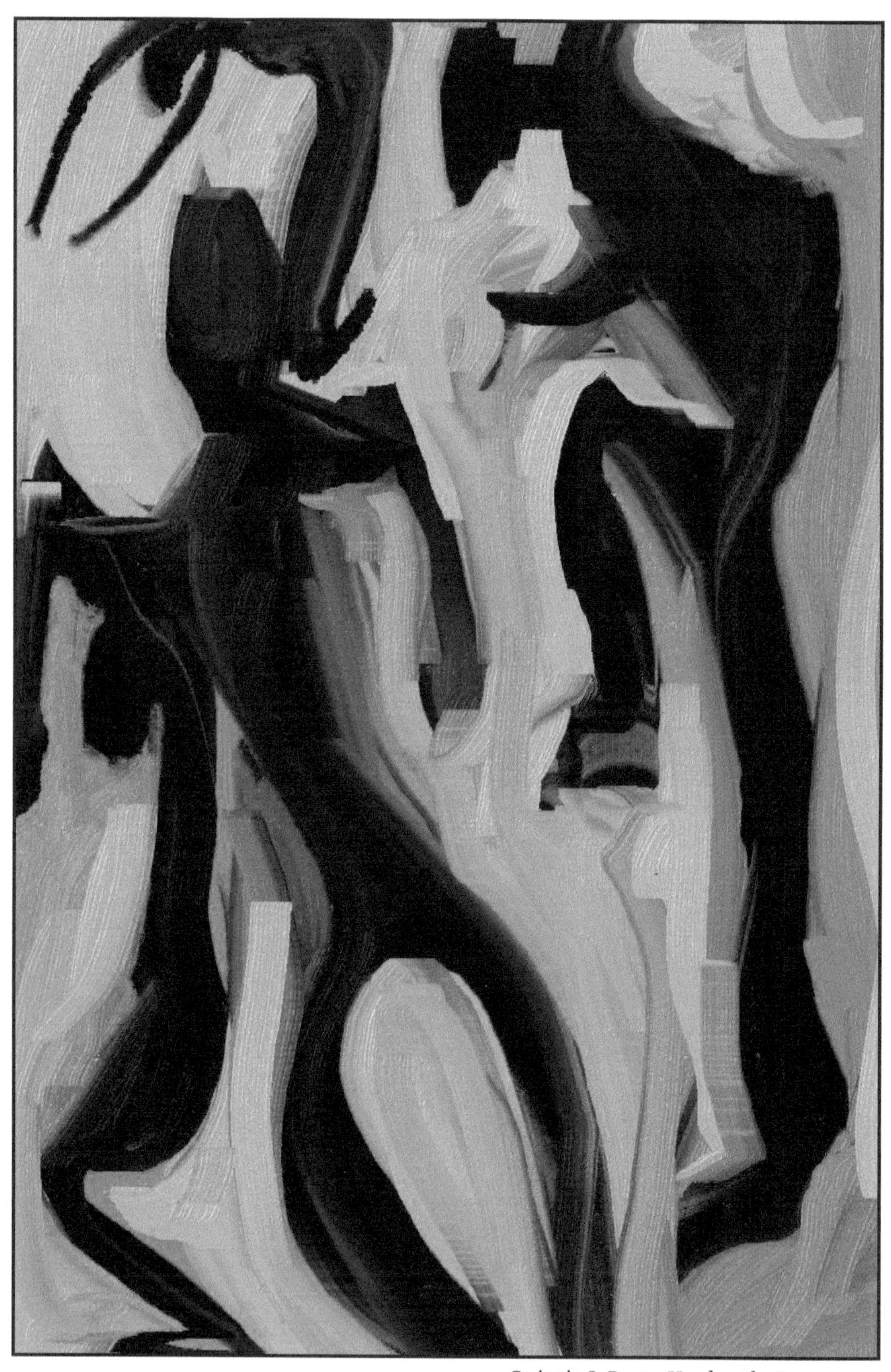

Swingin It Pretty Hard on the Dance Floor

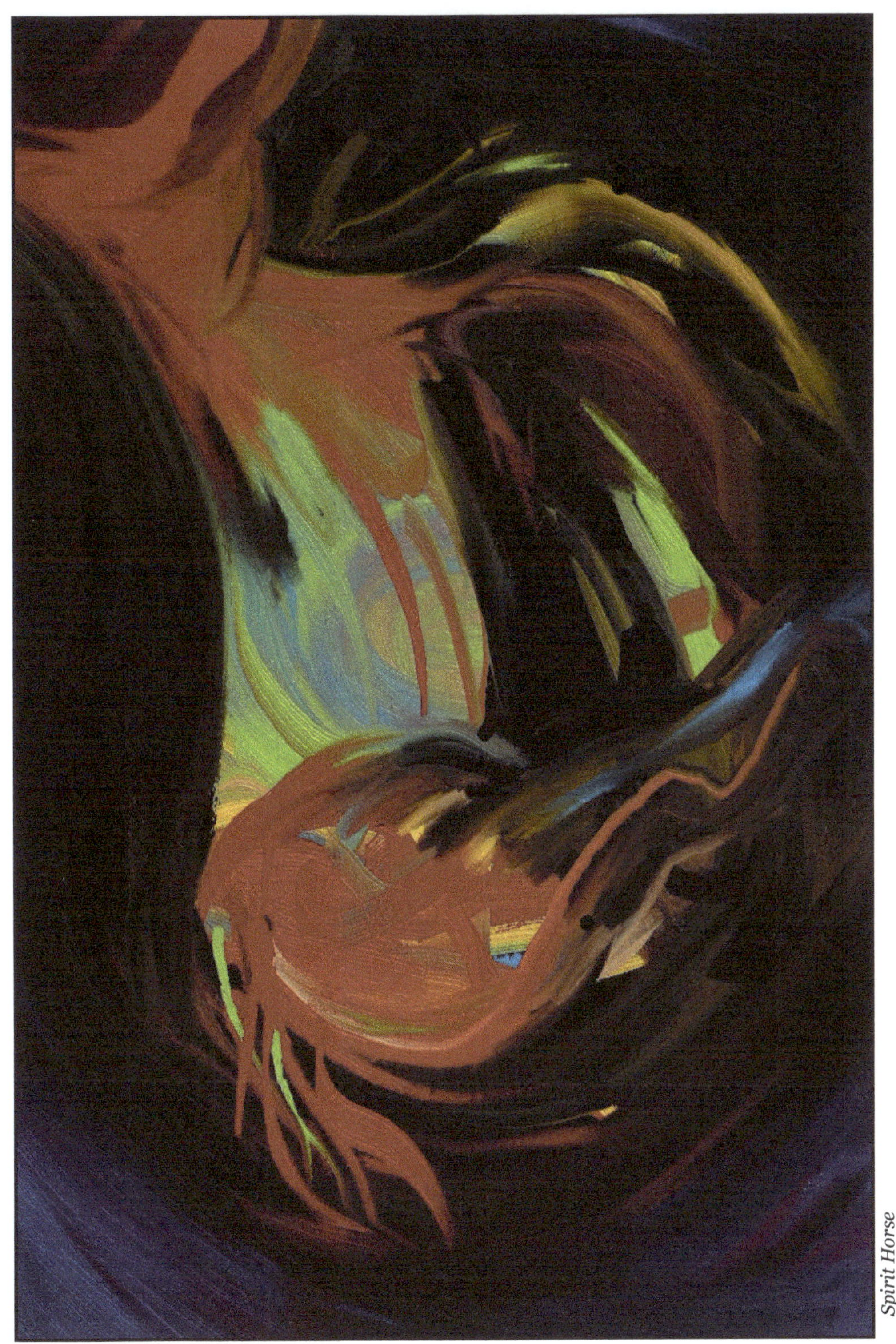

Spirit Horse

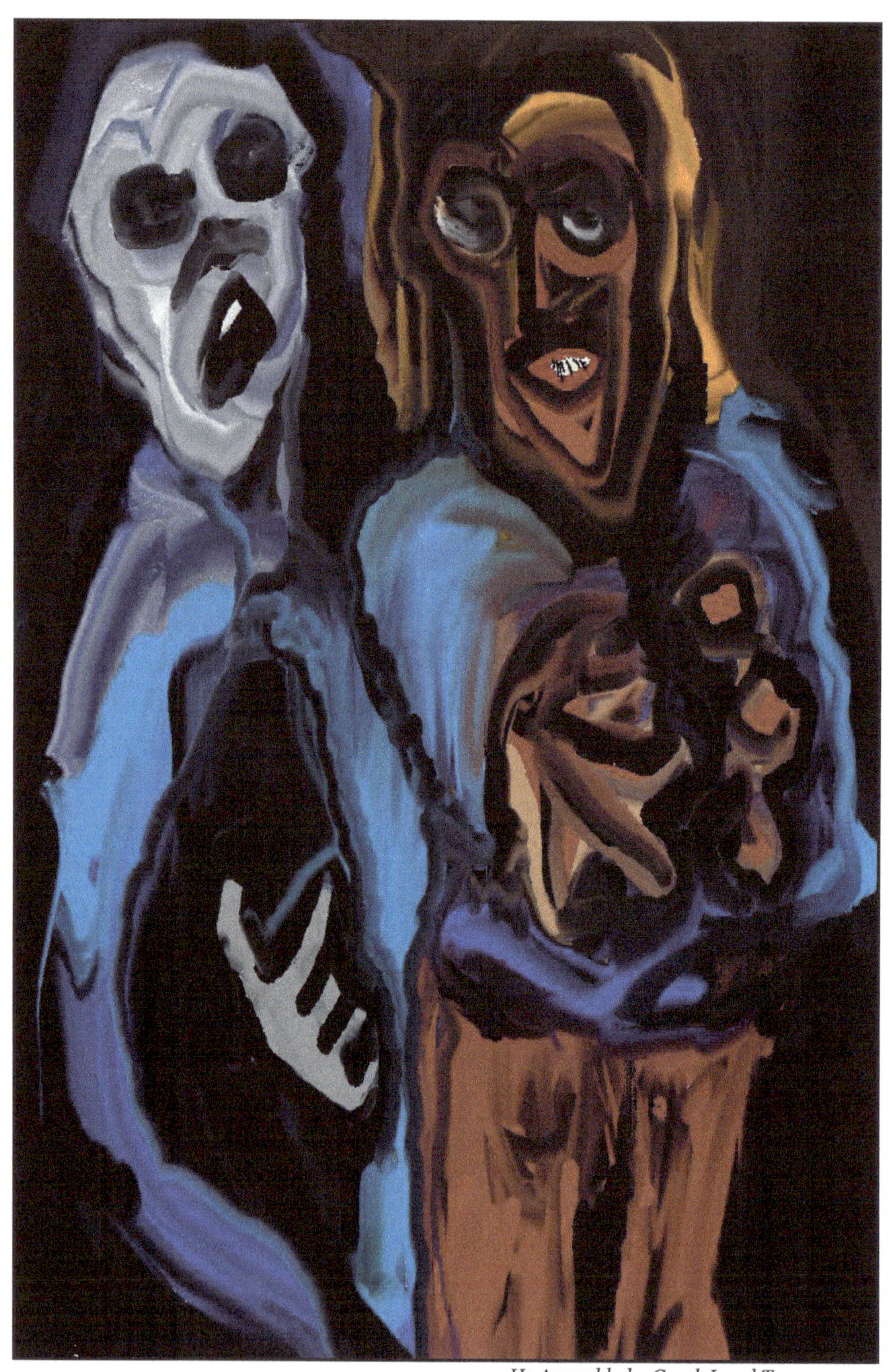

He Assembled a Crack Legal Team

On Memory

Mollie O'Leary

Lukewarm beer, tinny and prickly
on my tongue at 8 years old.
My sister and I used to steal sips

of foam when dad turned
to kiss the other goodnight
in one of his better moods.

We would listen for footfalls,
measured and sharp like
the drawing of blood,

and hurriedly bury ourselves
under blankets before he threw
open the door in one of his other moods.

Through a small space
in the covers, we could glimpse
each other's fate.

Memory is slippery
like a spill on the floor
that I rush to cover up

because being
someone's child
carries consequences:

Of all my children,
I thought you would have it
in your heart

to forgive me.
You are the most
like your mother.

Cherry

Ella Rous

I pressed my face inward,
into a facsimile of dried cherry—
let it drift, flat and withered, into the other salamander dust.
I am not gone. My fingerprints left grooves in the metal wall
of your abhorred chest.

For you, I cut off my tongue and placed it
on the asphalt at the Texas poolside.
You didn't want it, but you did, all the same.
You were lying flat. I watched, with precise incaution,
the loving snakes make taffy of your nomadic skin,
and wrap themselves inside.
You laughed at me: "something's different" and smashed
your matchstick elbows across the concrete.

My appetite smallens under your watchful emptiness.
The energy in its never-destruction becomes
the heat storm in my heart and hands.
Nothing will come of nothing:
lightning is choked into silence by cold,
gossamer fingers.

Mania is Fun

Sasha Torchinsky

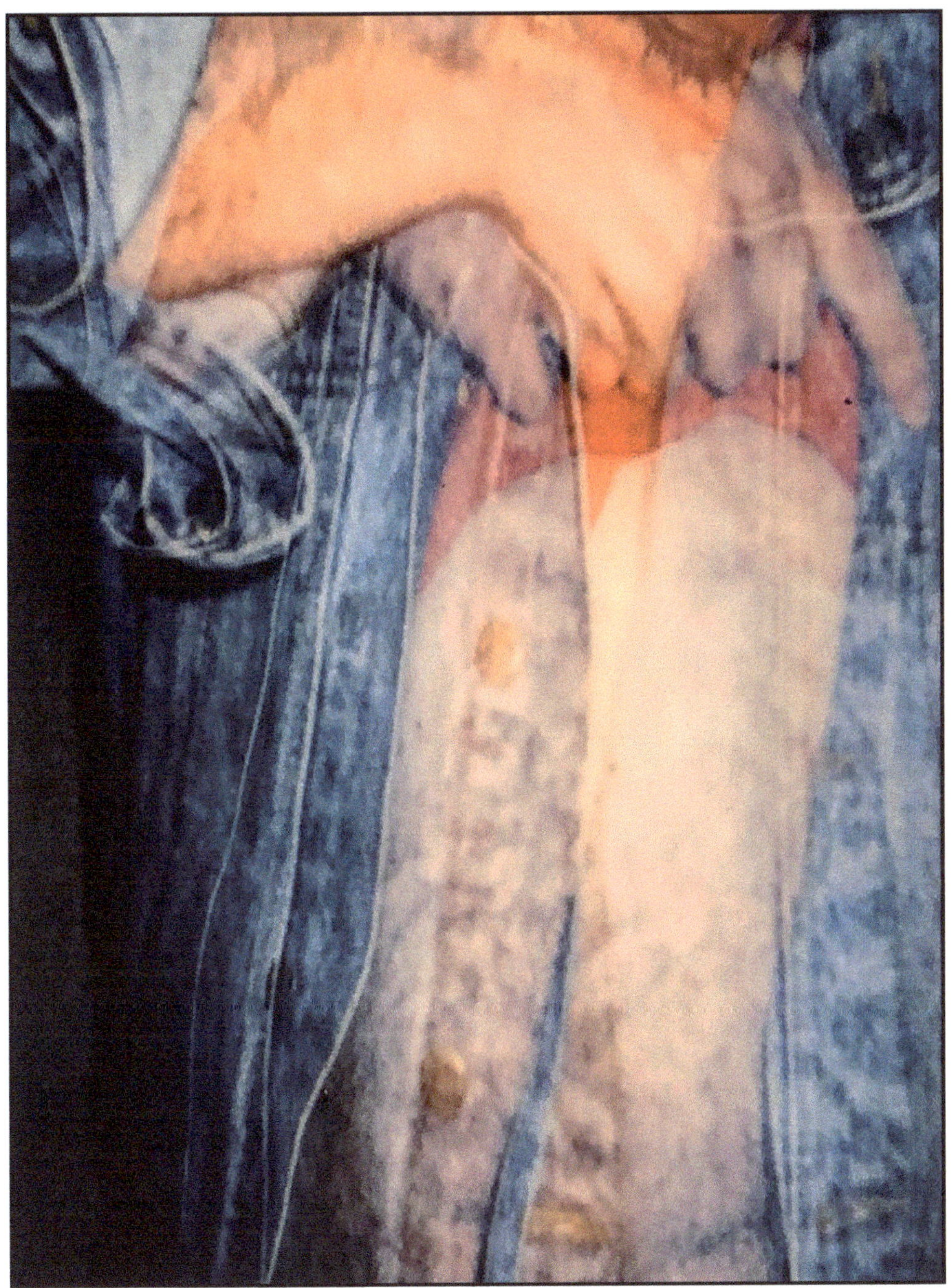

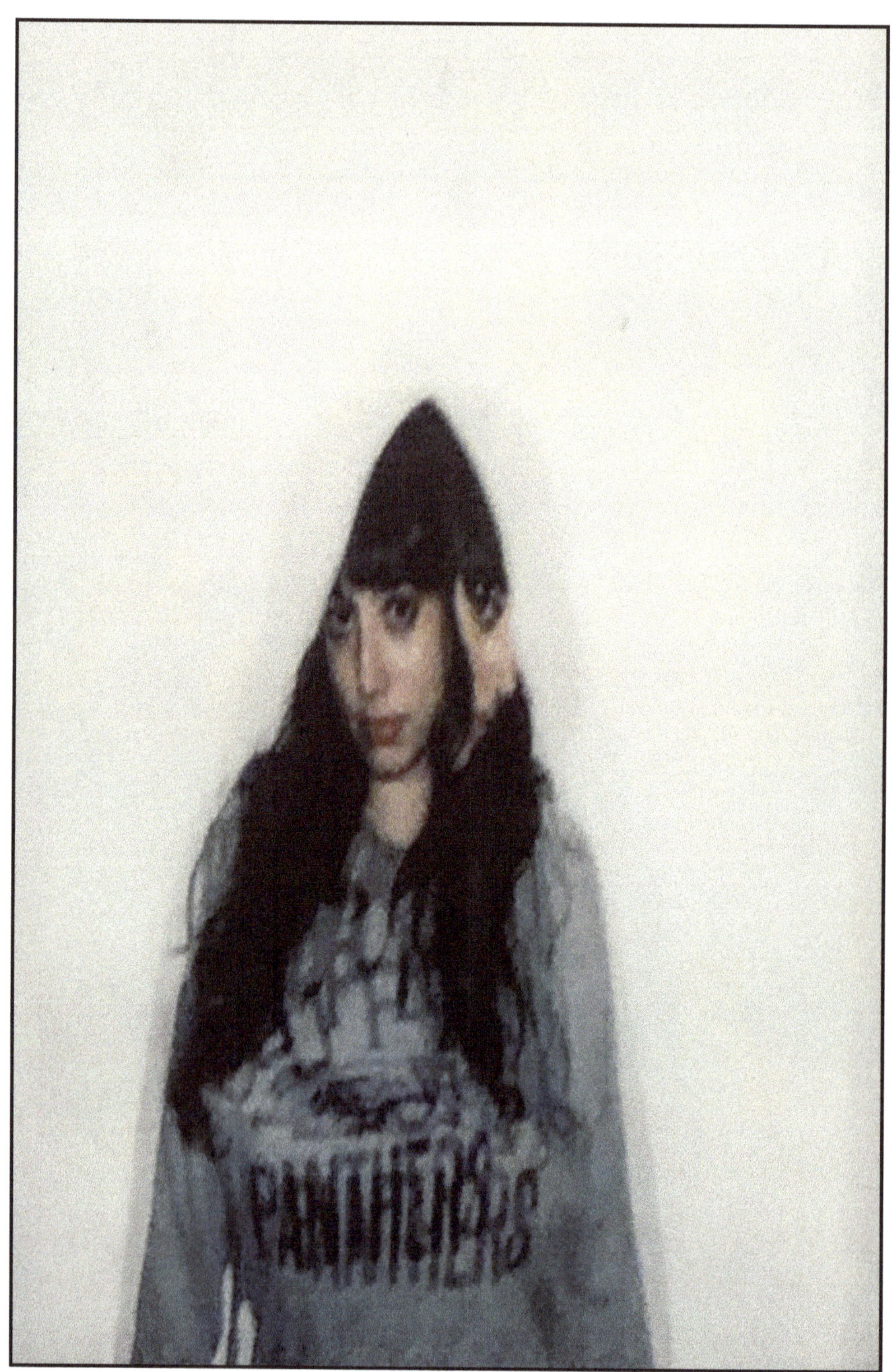

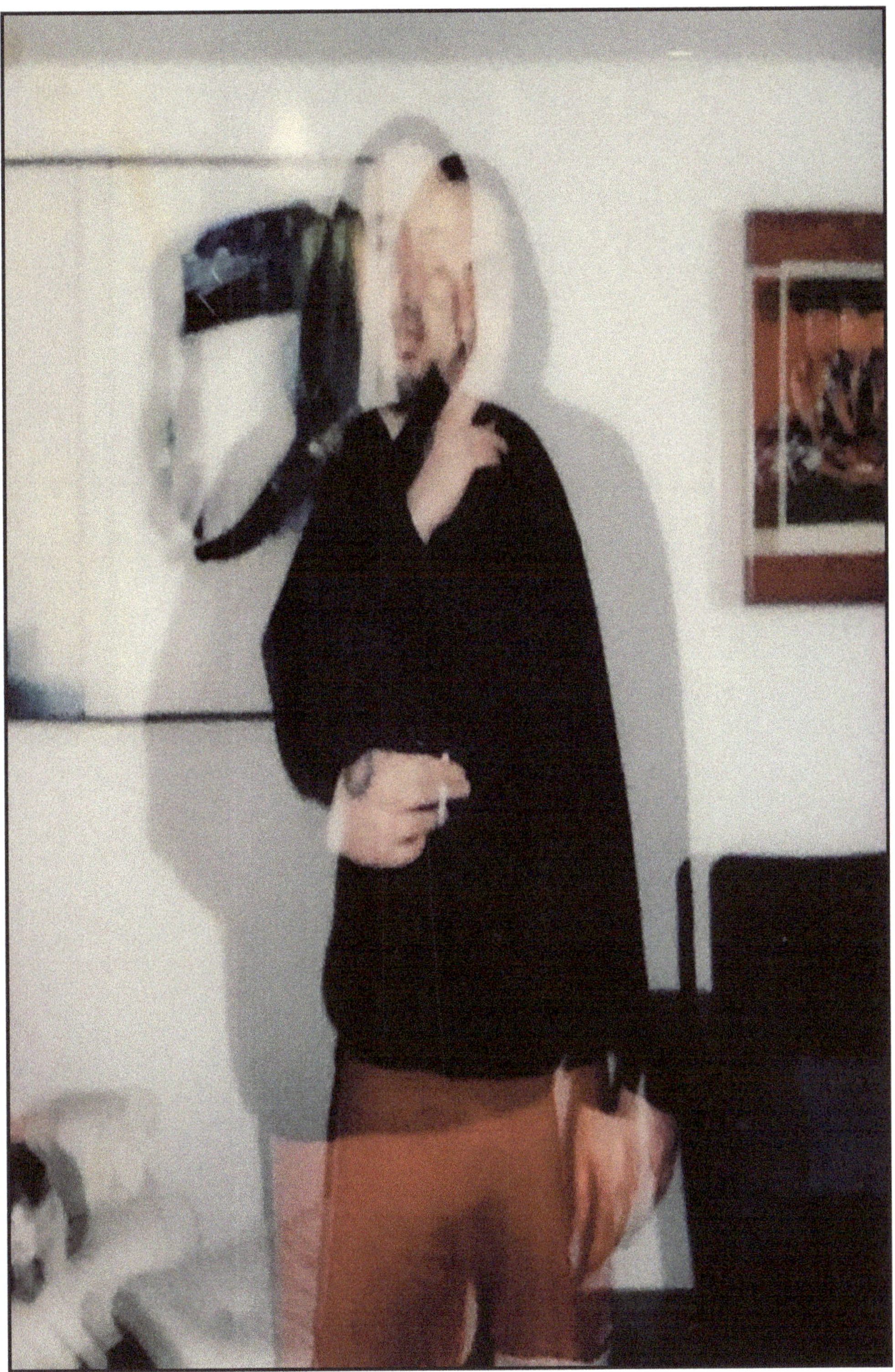

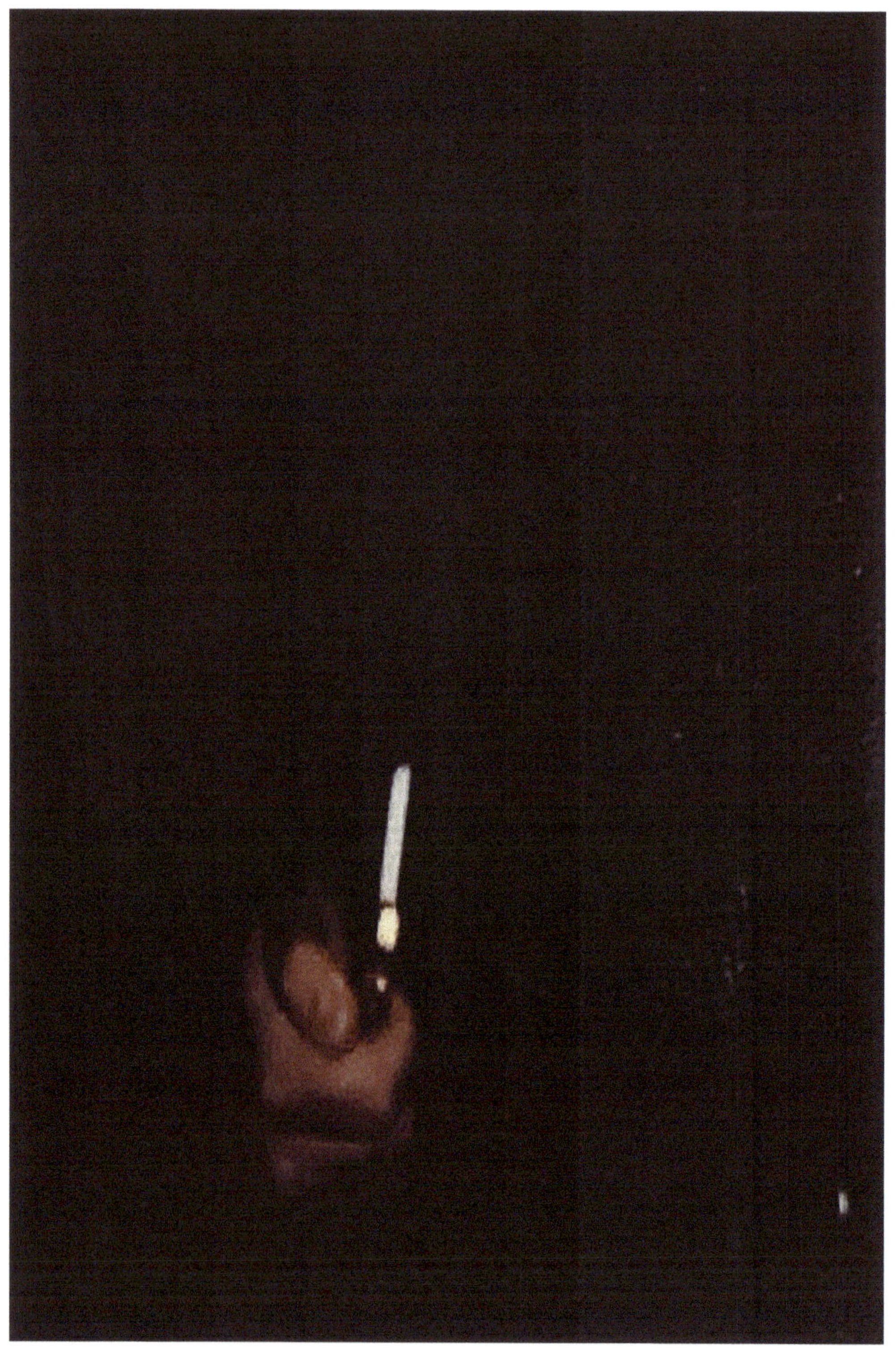

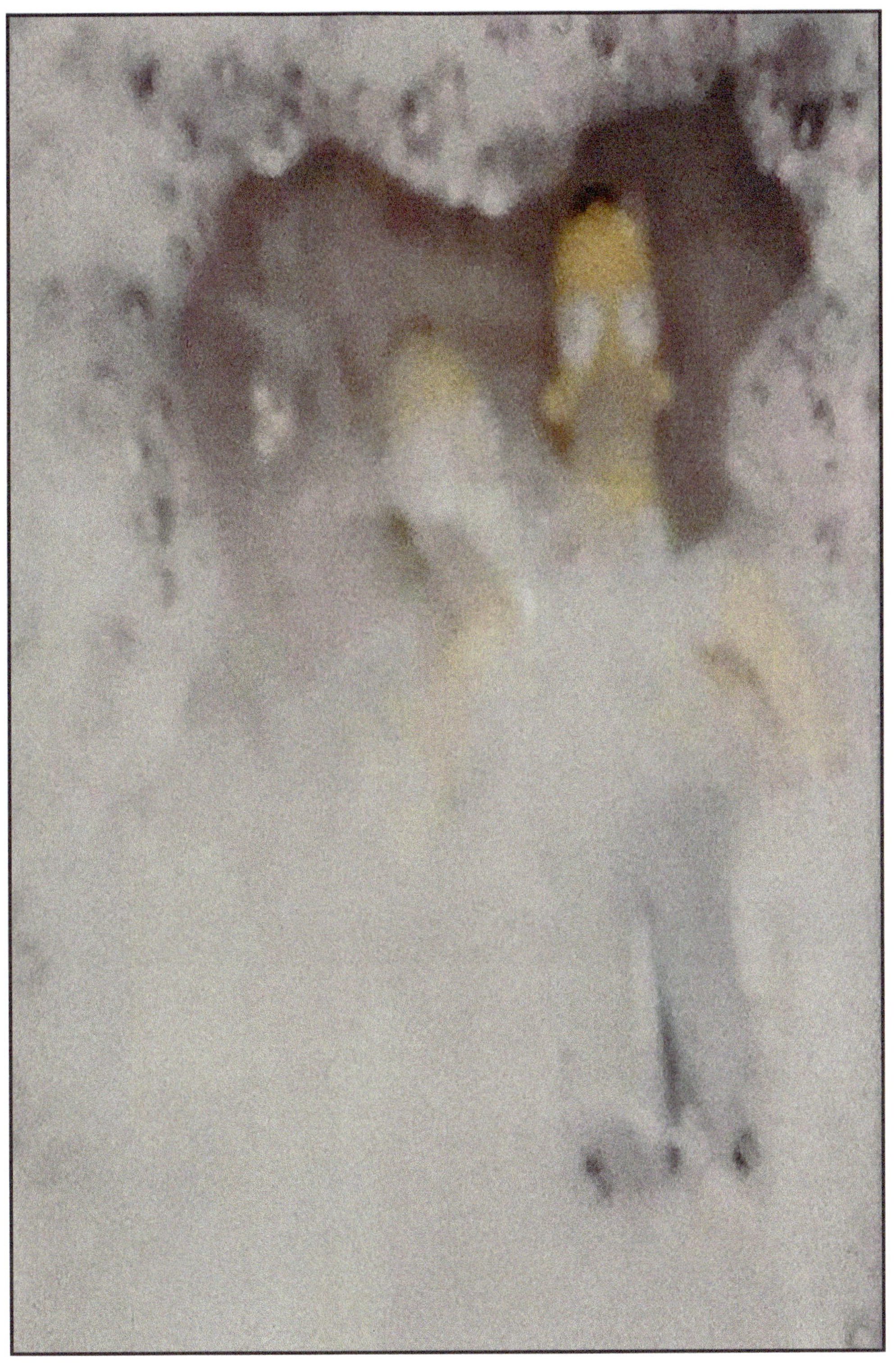

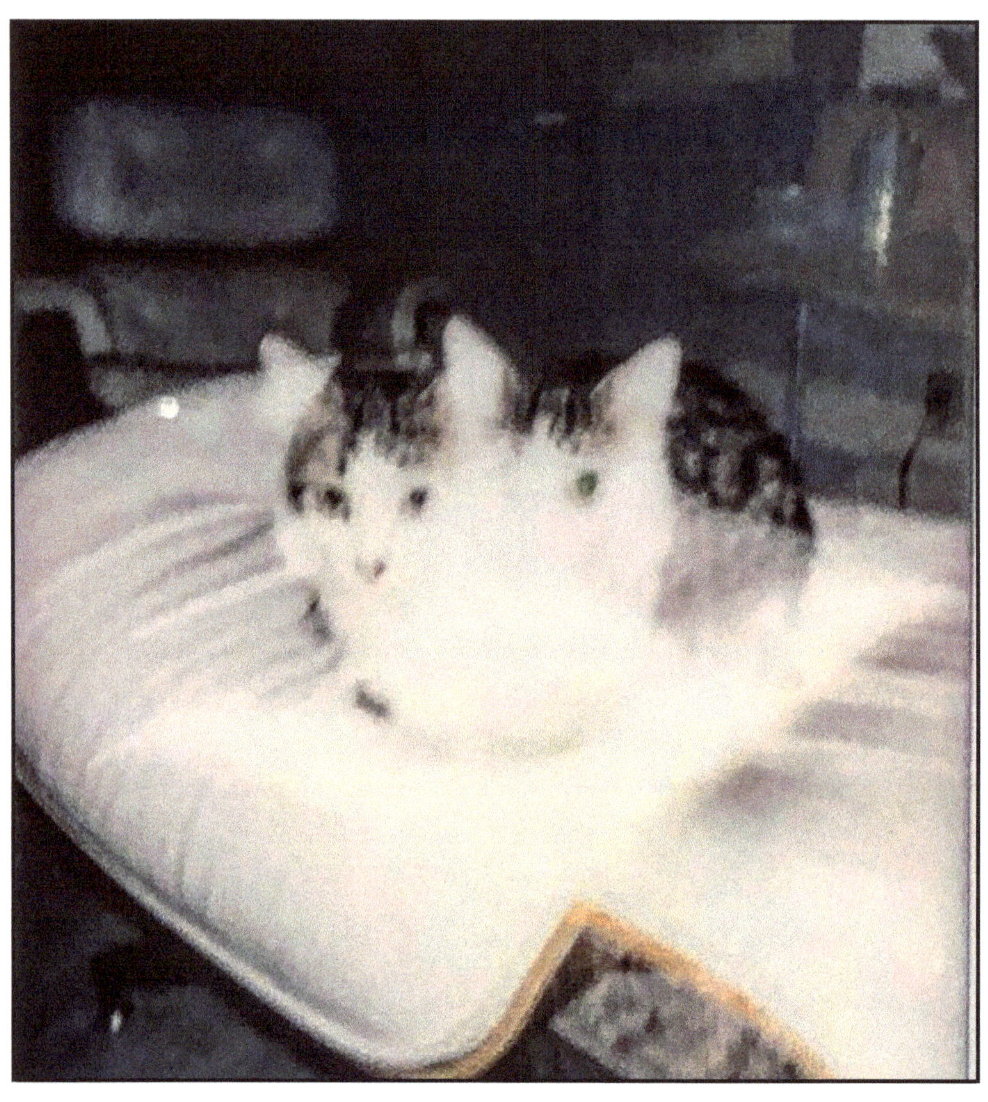

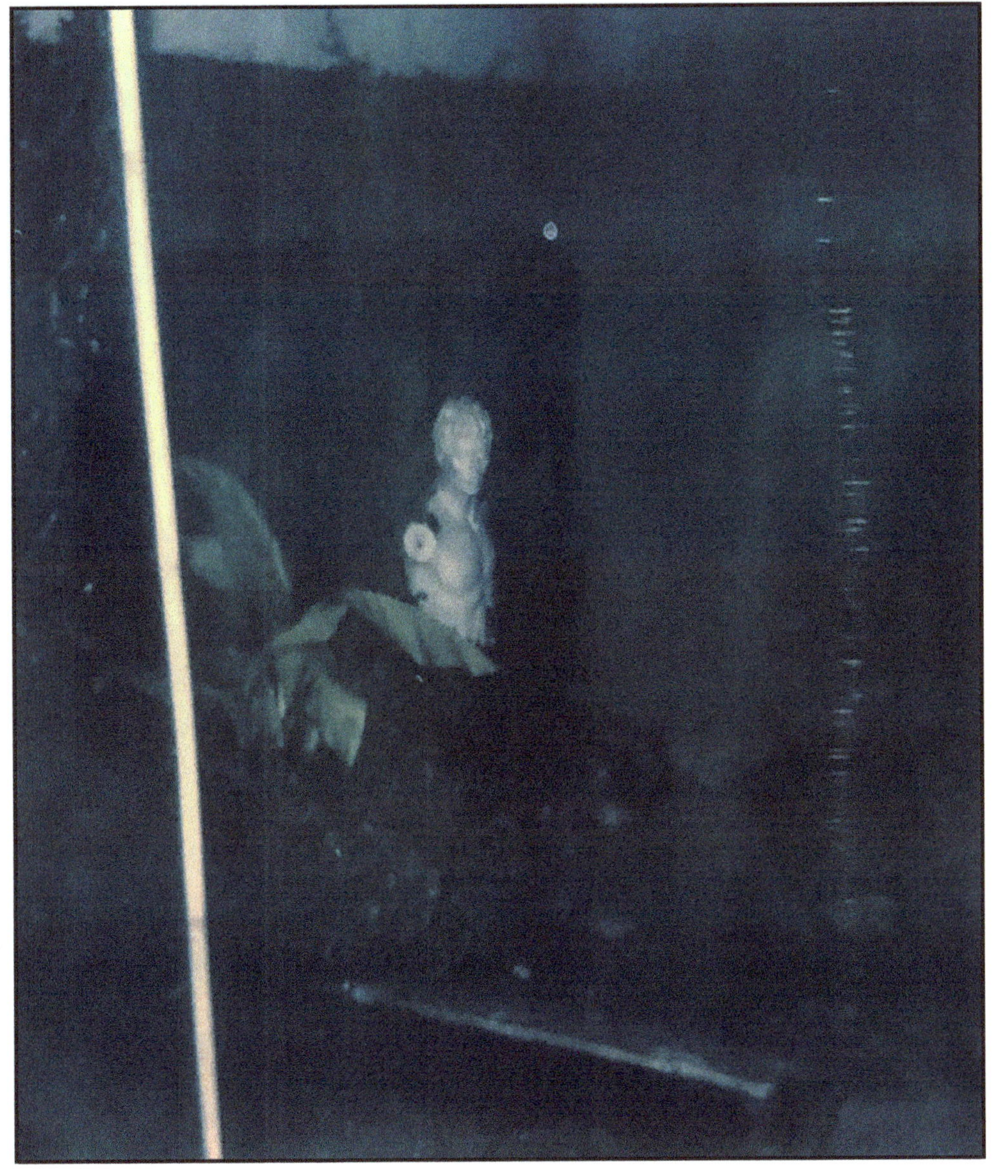

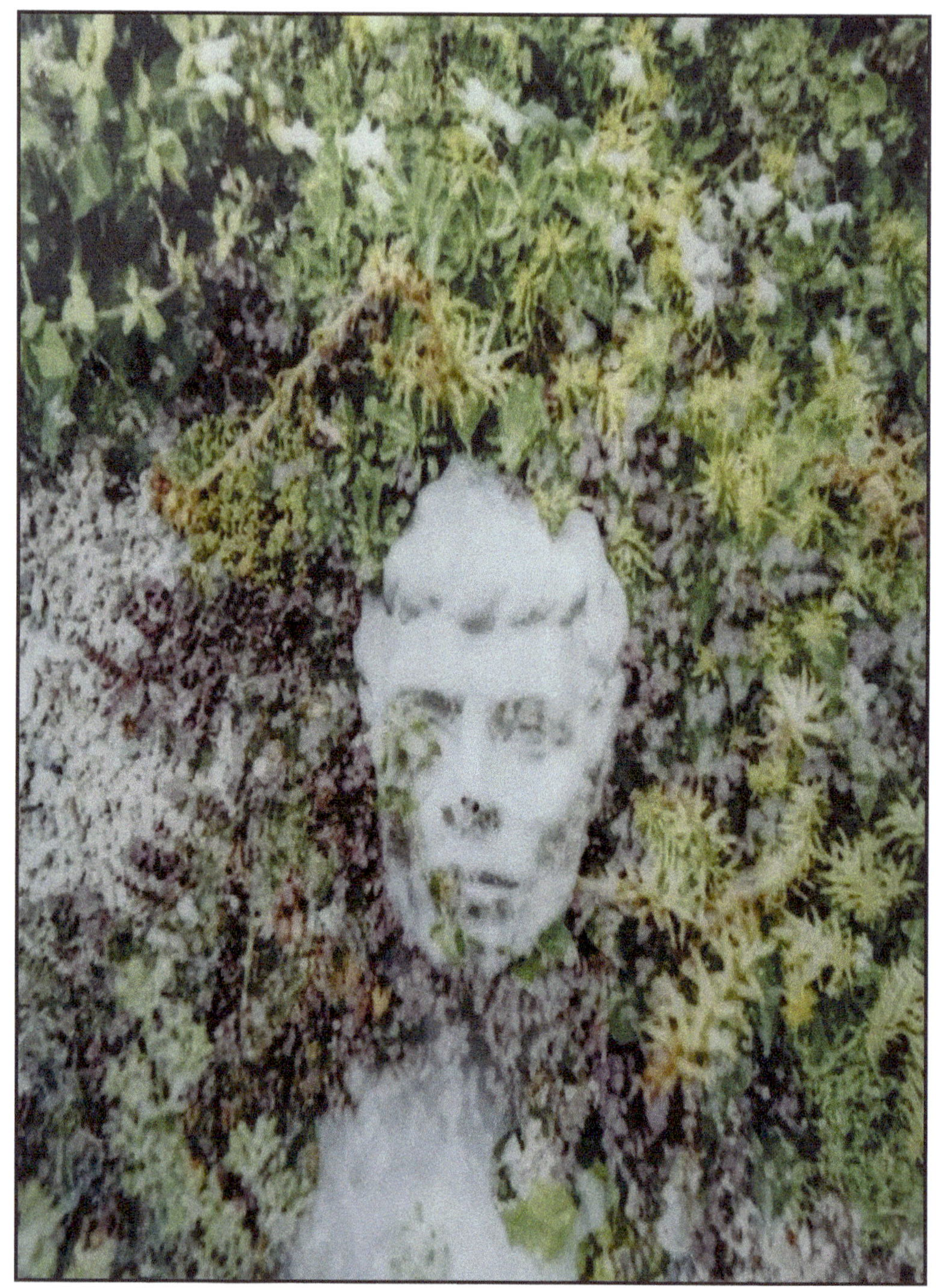

Fourth-Dimensional Gods Can't be Blamed for Climate Decay

Eros Livieratos

The trees in Alaska are growing drunkenly—
permafrost melts. Politicians profit. The wind beneath
your thighs is thick, with particulars—I stand in heat,
slicing tendon and breast; I wish to be a spiral. A pyramid
mangled, inverted—four-dimensional gods reach third
base in golden twine spun from dumpsters in New Jersey
overflowing with poison ivy and narcissus; nymphaea, and
bronzed lilium—bury me alive. A floral bed, ring around
the rosy—pools of love crosshatched behind chain-linked
habitats. A rainbow is a gun, a cop is an abuser. Rosacea skies
are fire trodden viking funerals of a time mourned future-present.
The ring around your finger
is a conflict mineral—I want it in my mouth.

All or Nothing

Sebastian Correa

We are so bored with our lives. We have it all: money before hitting our forties, professional accomplishments, and what everyone it seems strives for—leisure time. Yet here we are sitting across from one another, our coffee table book, *Post-Modern Nihilistic Endeavors of Subaltern Anti-Imperialist Post-Colonial Literary Theorists: A Case Study into Lacanian Freudian-Adjacent Paradigms in Subdialetic Post-Marxian Focaultian Pre-Baudrillard Post-Irigaray Justice Narratives: A Case Study in Social Constructivism Outside White Heteronormative Linguistic Post-Coital Machinations: A Case Study in—Are You Still Reading This Title?*, placed right on the table, staring at our screens.

"What are you doing?" I ask my wife as I type a message to—I already forgot.

"Yeah" she replies as she stares at her screen.

It wasn't always like this. We once had a fire, as individuals and as a couple.

"I'm so fucking bored!" I yell so loudly all her hair falls out. I stare at my wife, now bald and eyebrowless. She finally puts her phone down and produces a samurai sword. I get up and summon two little daggers.

"I hate you because I hate my life!" she yells, and in one motion she chops off my head. It grows back. So does her hair. There is just no conflict. Life is so arduously monotonous and boring. So we make an unspoken plan, to have fun again by hurting each other.

I jump into the air and backflip onto my chair. My wife pulls out an AK-47 out of her ass and begins to shoot me. I fall back; blood splatters everywhere. I front flip forward and land on both feet while simultaneously hurling both daggers that pierce through her skull.

"I blame you for making me bored and unhappy!" I scream as I watch blood trickle down her face. We both fly into the sky blowing a hole through our mansion's roof, Spanish terracotta tiles suspended in the air before crashing down onto the ground.

She shoves a nuclear bomb warhead down my esophagus. I fart out the explosion killing most of our neighbors. We look down and realize that maybe we could have fun by hurting others instead of each other. Maybe then we can feel whole again.

We deliver death to all our surviving neighbors: Susie Thompson walking her baby (both speared), Gavin McGines cheating on his wife with a male hooker (wife's already dead, for Gavin we summon a demon to behead him, hooker we let go and tip him like proper liberals but then he dies from the radiation. Watching his skin bubble and head burst and then bones transmute to chalk almost made my wife and I want each other again sexually), and our ethnically ambiguous banker neighbor Donde Esta-La-Substancia (we just bludgeon them [their gender is also ambiguous] to death with the smooth rocks we collected on a riverbed on our trip to the Hindu Kush back when we loved one another) who is tending to their rock garden unaware of all the death around them because they are wearing AirPod headphones.

Killing rich people, we realize, isn't that fun. So we make an unspoken agreement: to kill the poor, the brown, the already suffering. Surely we will find meaning in that.

We fly to the Bronx and bomb entire housing projects watching the people flee their huge urine-drenched-at-the-base buildings only for us to launch lighting bolts, zapping them, watching them from the sky, their bodies curling up like dried, crispy ethnic ants under a sun powered magnifying glass.

We realize that killing American poors just isn't as fun as *real* poors. We want to see bloated brown bellies, and flies and vultures waiting for a child to die of starvation, and mud huts and mud roads and frowns on muddy faces hiding under regal palm trees, to be enriched by the cultural experience like the sophisticated cosmopolitans that we are.

So we go to the third world and peel the skin off the bodies of crying babies, transform into the very nightmarish folkloric monsters that these people fear; we reign terror on little villages nestled inside jungles, deserts, canyons, grasslands, but my dick still doesn't get hard; my wife still doesn't' laugh, and we still don't experience the euphoria of what it means to truly be alive.

Back home, sweating from a day of hard, fruitless labor, we look into each other's eyes for what seems like the first time, and a tsunami of realization washes over us: we each need to hurt ourselves in order to feel whole again.

So I stab my face for half an hour. My wife bathes in hydrochloric acid while drinking and inhaling hydrofluoric acid. I slit my throat. She gives herself a mastectomy.

"I hate myself!"

"I hate myself more!"

I chop off my penis with a scimitar. She hangs herself with sustainable and fair-trade hemp rope. I bolt nails into my shins, thighs, and thoracic cavity. She self-immolates sitting in lotus position (an artistic homage to her favorite iconic picture: Vietnamese monk Thích Quảng Đức protesting by setting himself on fire while meditating).

But we just don't die. We are condemned to live. We all are.

Finally we give up.

"Want to watch Netflix while staring at our phones and ignoring each others presence and needs and feelings and company?" I ask my wife, taking a selfie.

"Yeah, cool," she says already reading an email and then sending a text.

Glimpses of a Fairy Tale

Monica Wiesblott

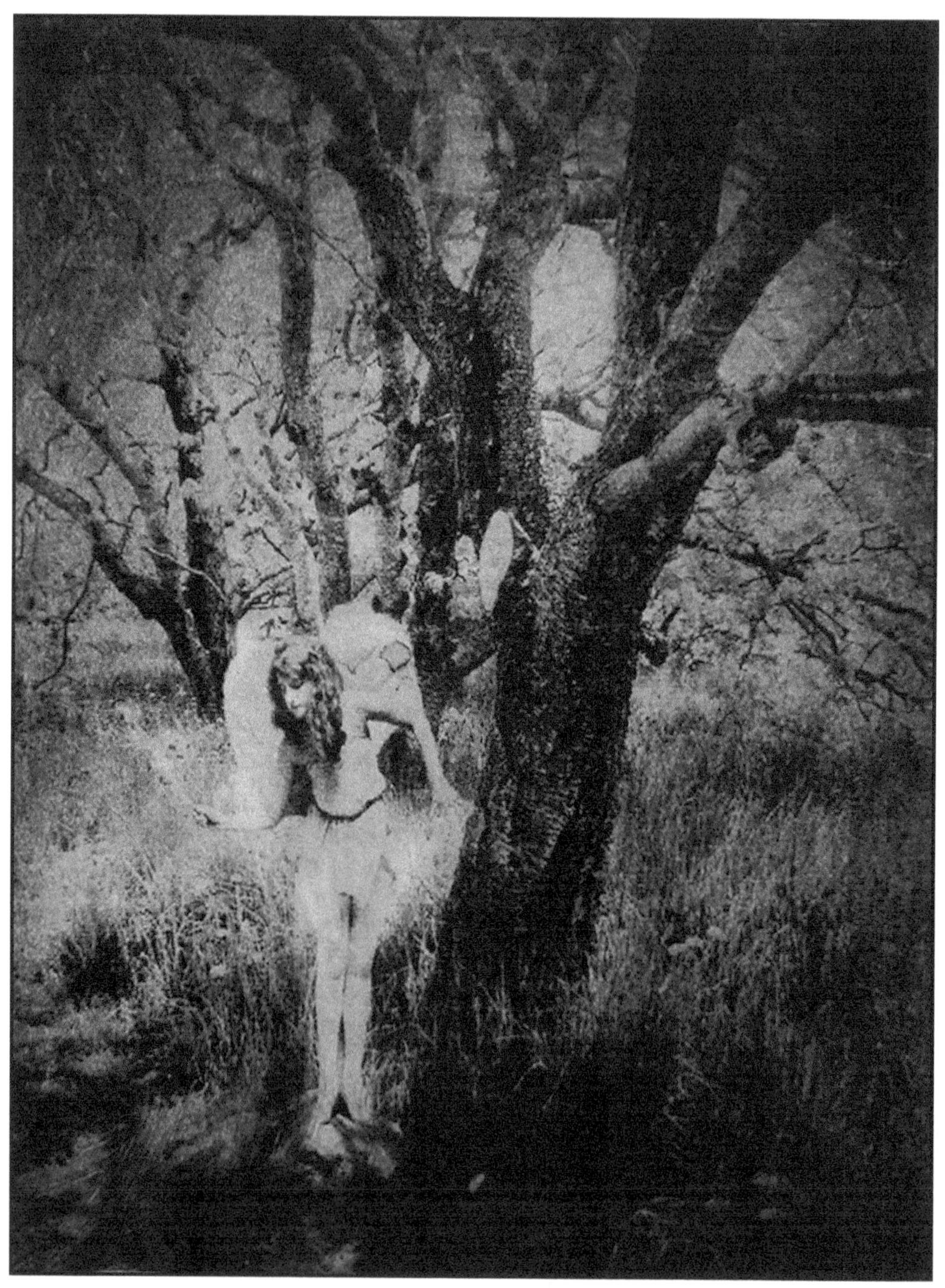

The Blue Fairy

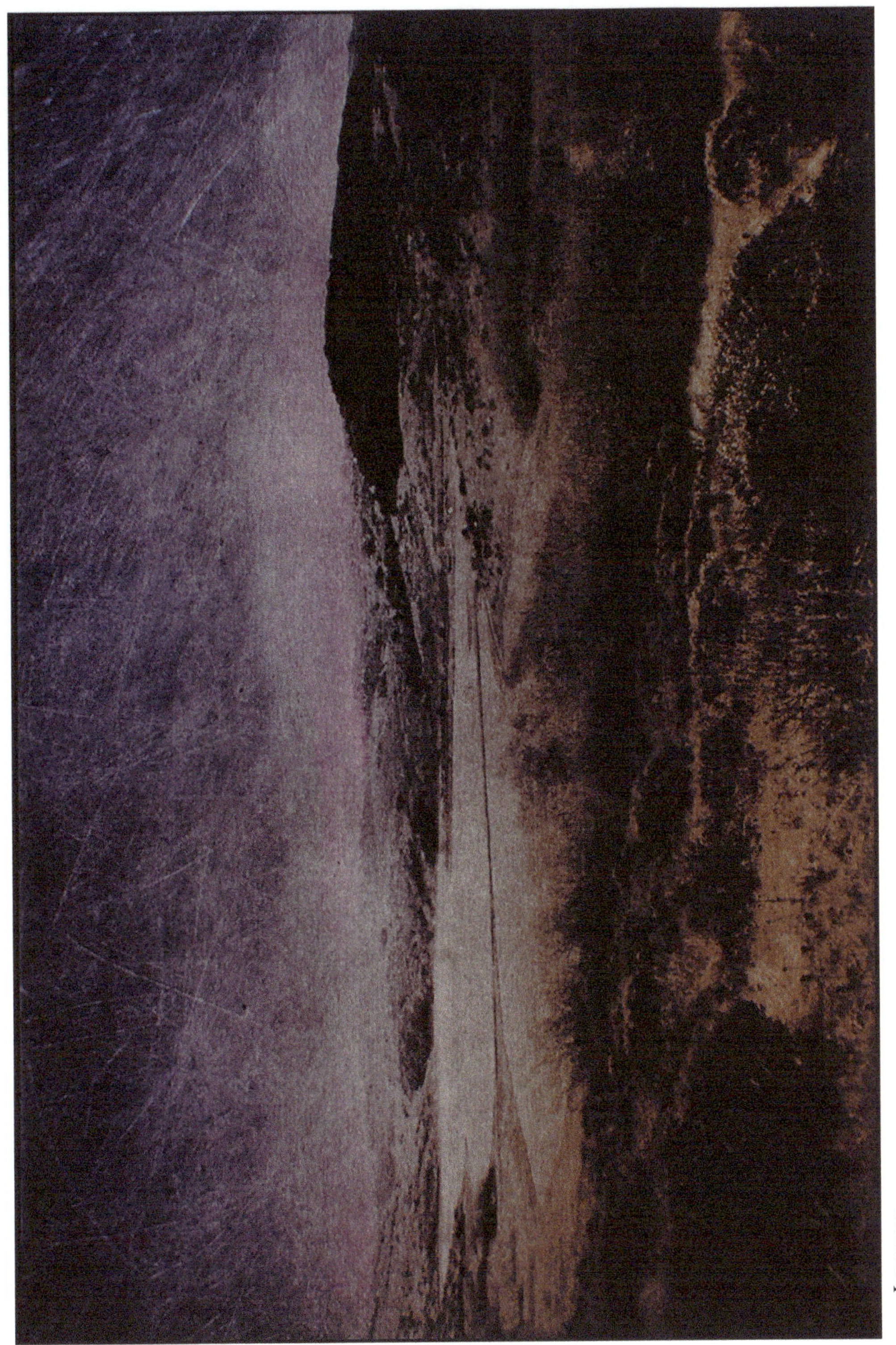

Inverness

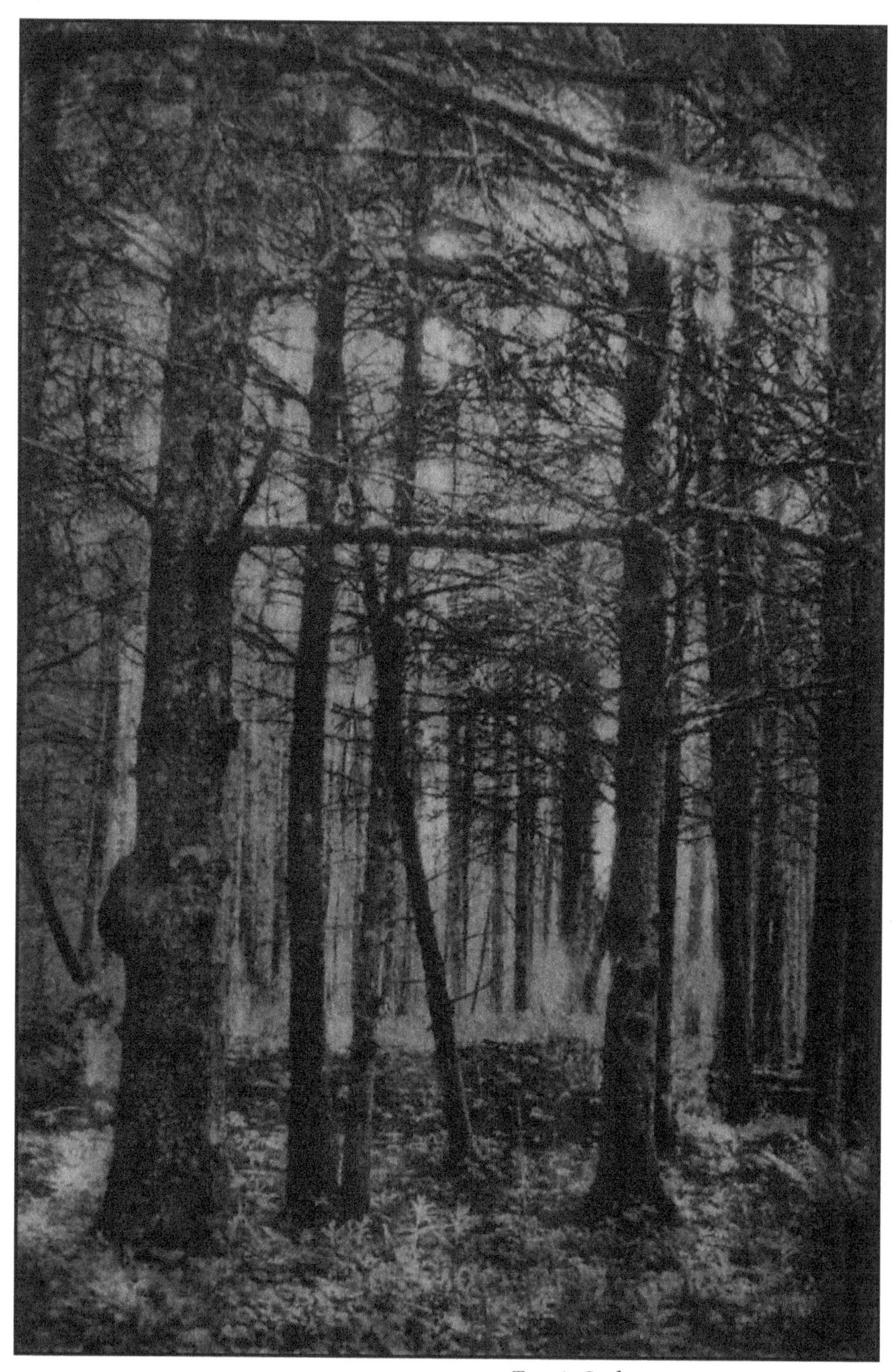

True As Sunbeams

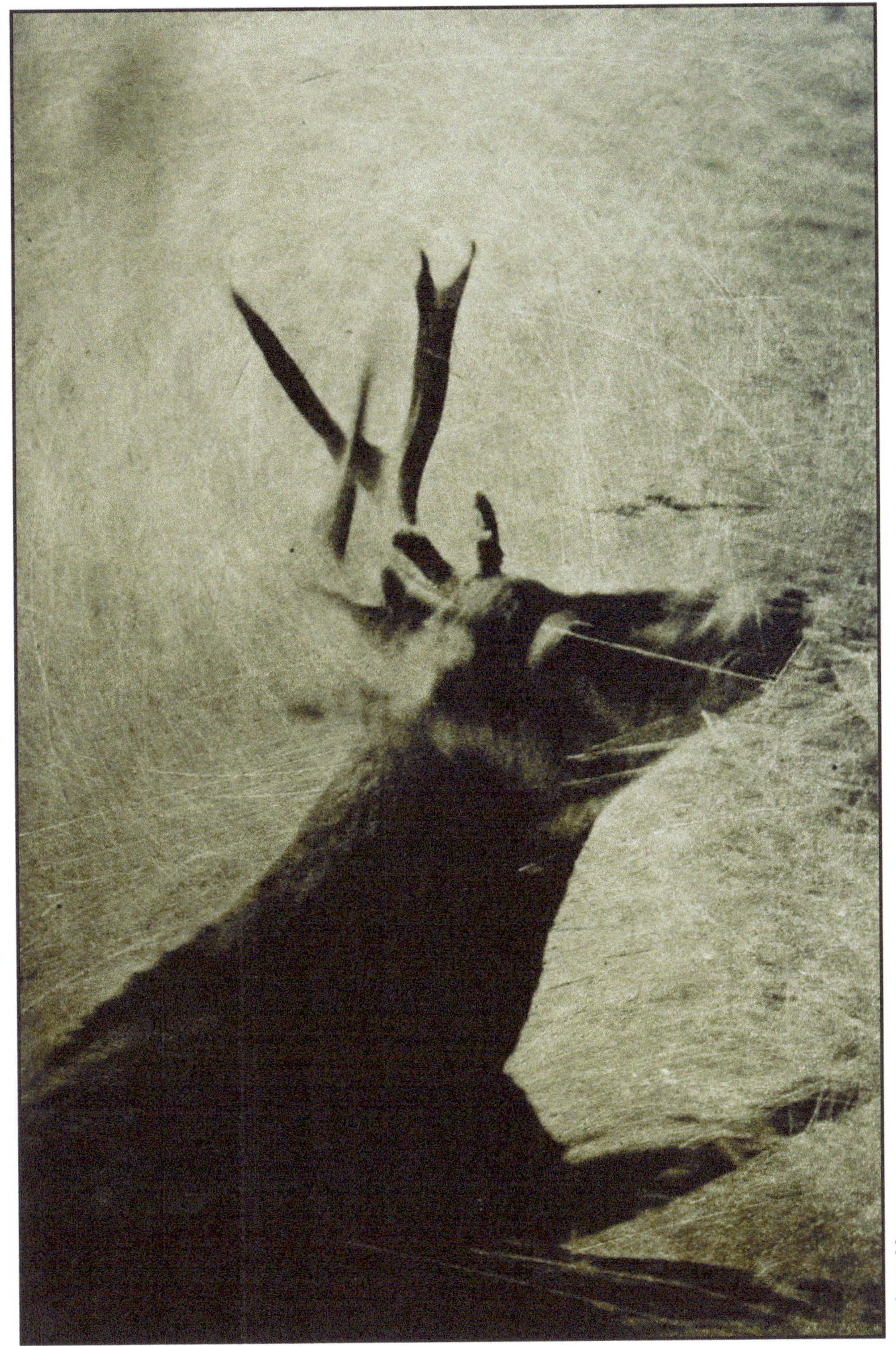

The Fable

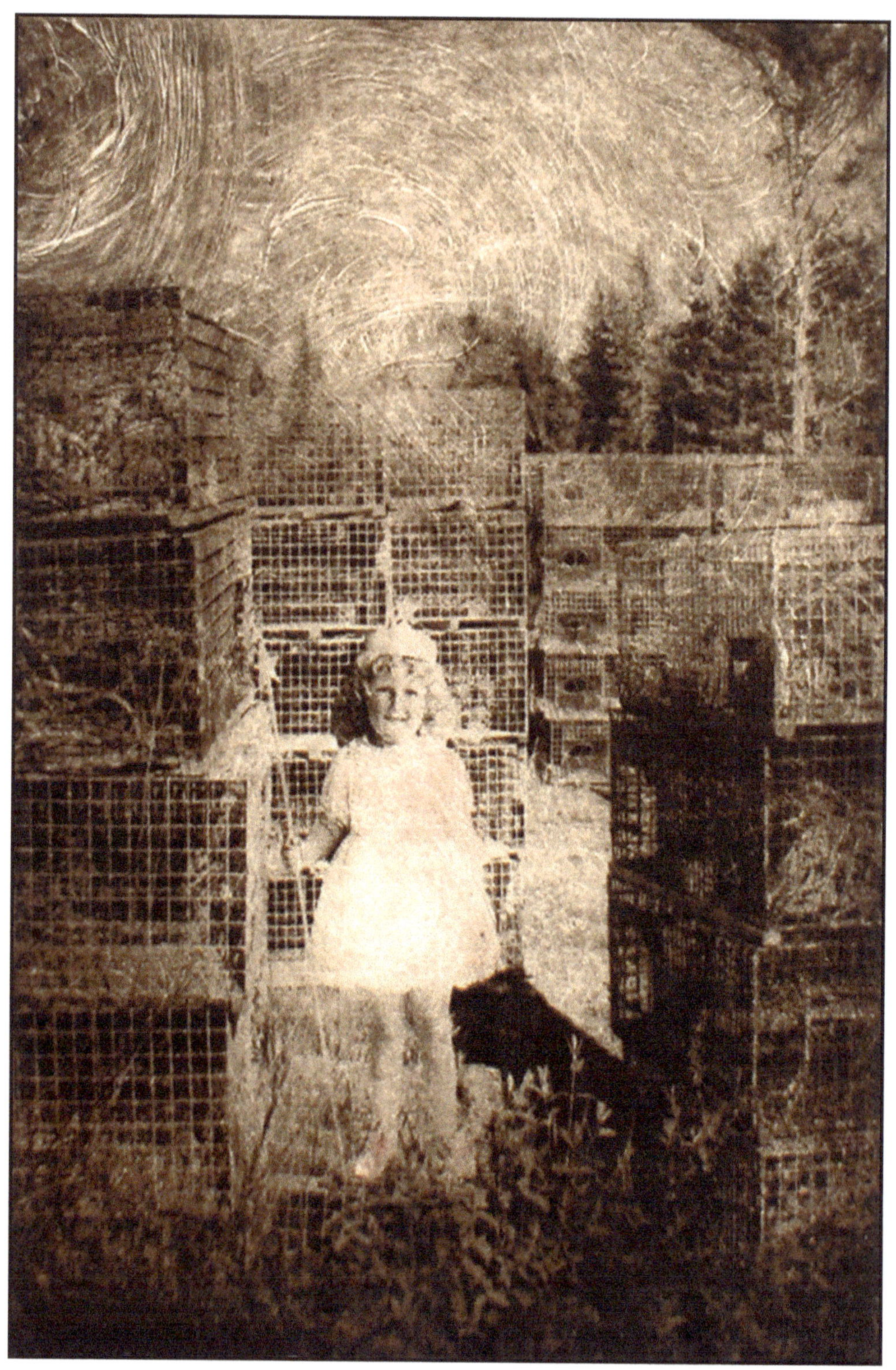

The Princess of Herring Gut

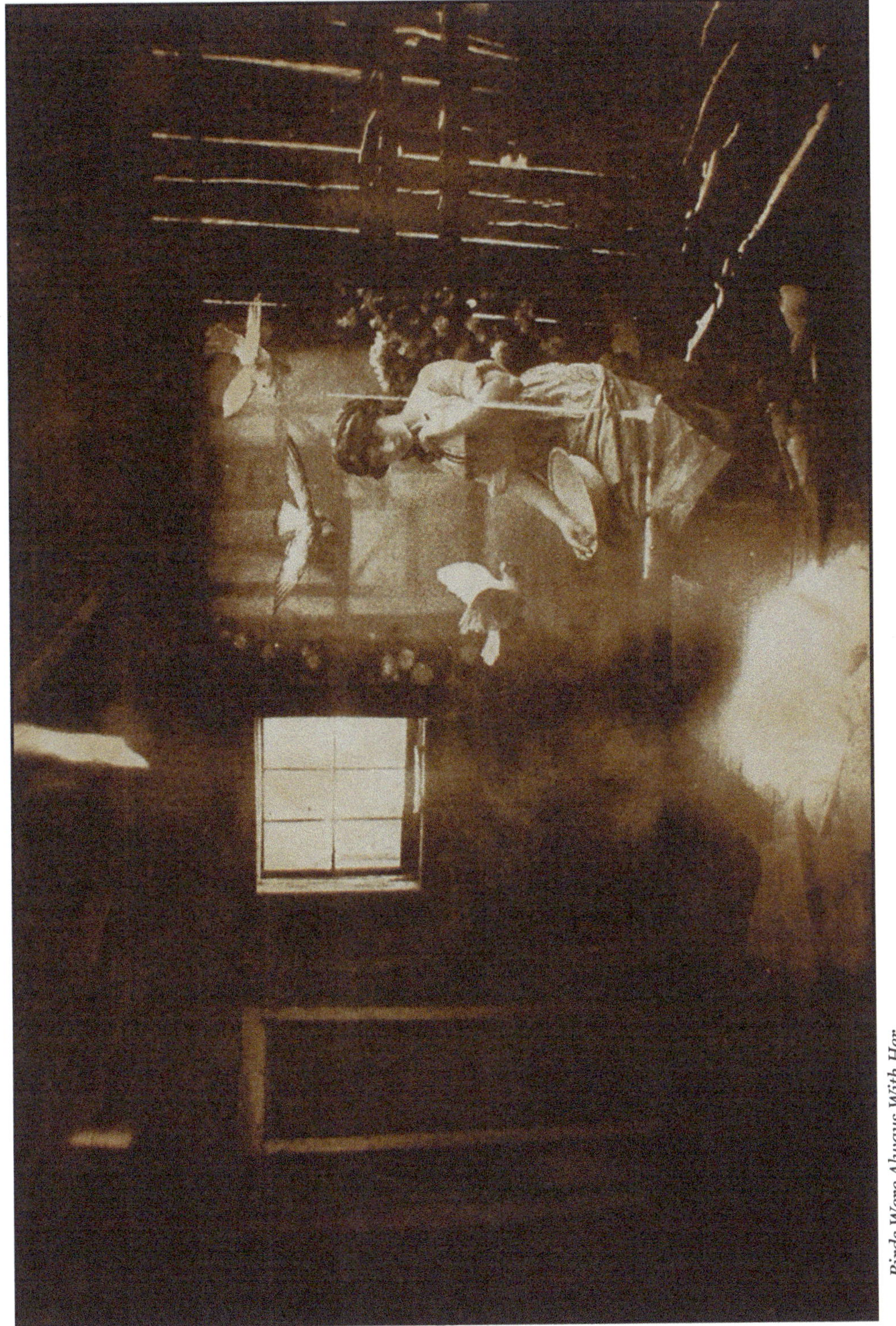

Birds Were Always With Her

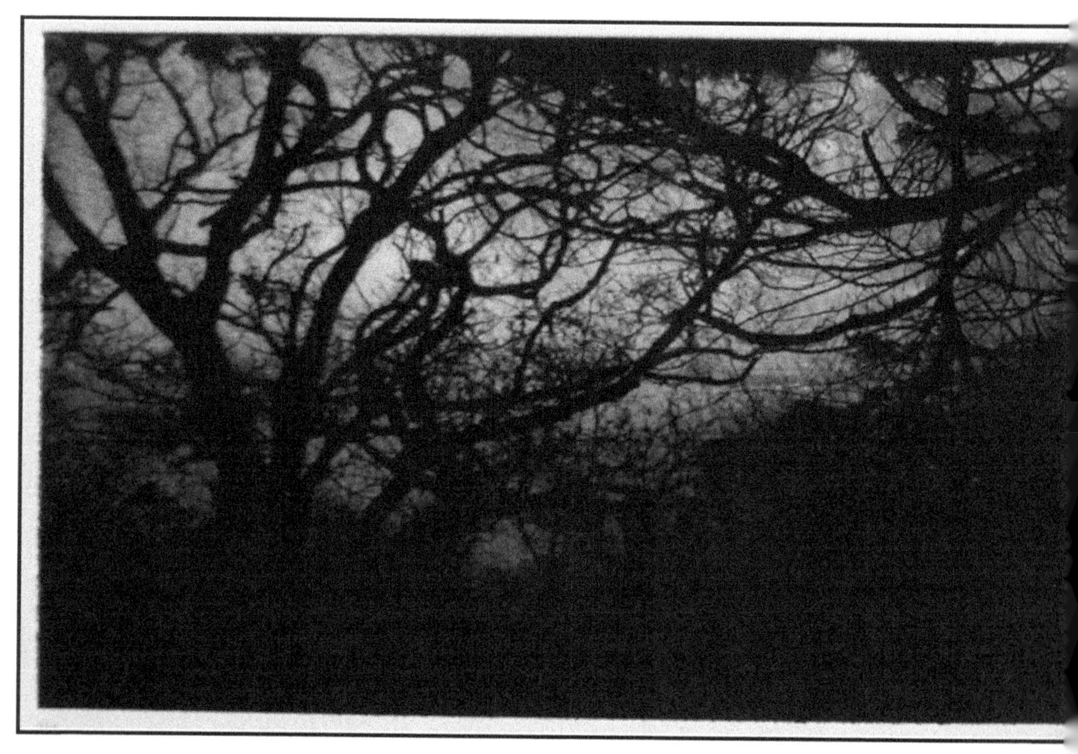

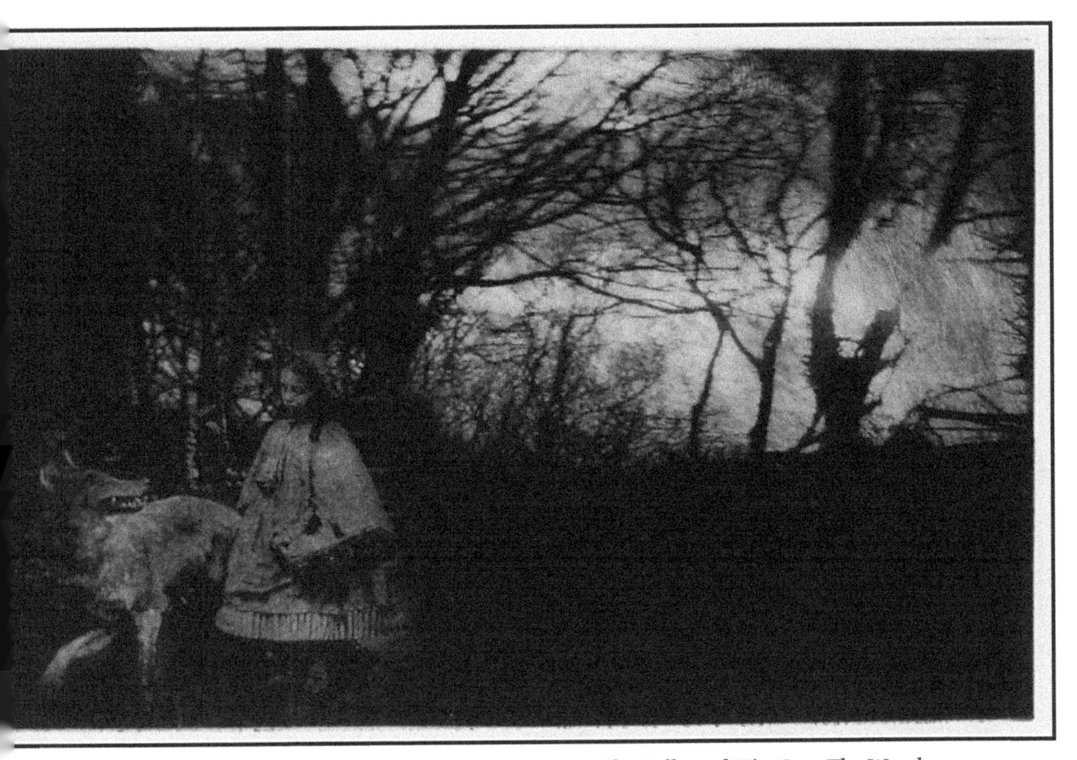

She Followed Him Into The Woods

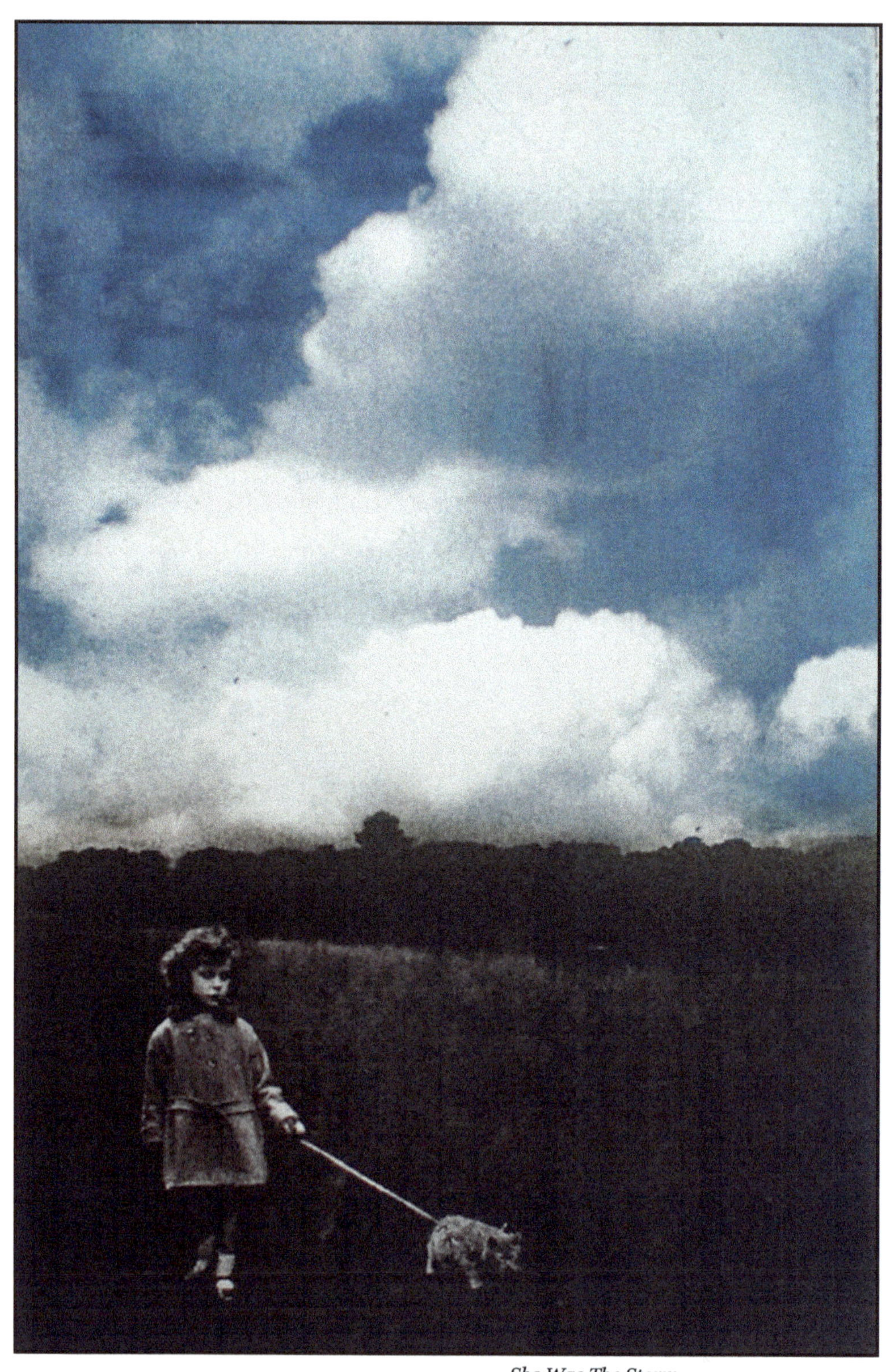

She Was The Storm

The Aviary

Matthew Gordon

Three kestrels perched in one tree, three vultures in the other. The vultures were not entirely fond of the forest setting, but getting the kestrels to agree to the meeting anywhere else would have taken weeks. Neither group of birds had the time to arrange an alternate meeting place. Much as the vultures would have preferred a more open area, they were well aware that the venue was not the most important aspect of the meeting.

The lone heron occupied a tree between them. It would have preferred a glade or wetland, but like the vultures, it had to defer to the wishes of the kestrels. Neither the vultures nor the heron planned to defer any longer, the vultures out of their interest and the heron out of the extraordinary power it wielded.

An enormous rat carcass lay prone on the grass. It was dead less than a day but would soon rot. The kestrels and the vultures both laid claim to it. The heron, which was a veritable pescatarian, had been called in to decide the issue. Each side had prepared its arguments since the moment of the rat's death, while the heron had not seen the carcass until only a few minutes earlier.

"It is quite the rat, I'll admit," murmured the heron as it stooped its neck downward.

"Enough for three meals, by my estimate," piped up a kestrel.

"Incredible," replied the heron. It paused, then asked softly yet authoritatively, "cause of death?"

"We killed it!" exclaimed another kestrel, puffing out its chest.

"It was old and fat," snapped a vulture. "Probably had a heart problem and died when it saw your ugly face."

"I hope you realize the irony of a vulture calling someone else ugly," countered the kestrel who had made the exclamation.

"Please, enough," said the heron. "As far as I am concerned, any bird other than a heron, crane, egret, swan or goose lacks a sufficiently attractive neck anyway."

"Fair enough," muttered a kestrel. "We did kill the rat, though, and that entitles us to it."

"We – are – vultures," one of the vultures, to this point silent, explained as if the kestrels were daft. "We are scavengers, not murderers. We claimed this *dead* rat and we believe it is ours."

The heron looked at the kestrels and then back over at the vultures, and then down at the rat. The kestrel was right. The rat more than likely contained just enough meat to feed either of the groups but not both.

"Is there some way to divide the rat?" inquired the heron. "You would all only get half a meal, but I am certain that you are all such capable hunters and scavengers that you would still manage to fill yourselves well before sunset."

A kestrel shook its head violently. "If we cut open the rat, its entrails will spill, and then there will be little left but ribs and rump."

It continued, "...the vultures might like that. Can they not eat carrion?"

"Carrion?" repeated the largest vulture, who was appalled by the question. "What do you think we are, buzzards? I will have you know we are dignified creatures that consume the deceased."

"Will either side accept compensation in return for the rat?" asked the heron. "Perhaps another animal to be determined at a future date?"

"This rat is too valuable," said a kestrel and a vulture nearly in unison. "It is the largest we have ever seen, and we are hungry now."

The heron sighed. The kestrels and vultures sat nearly motionless on their branches but for their incessant fuming.

"This is not productive," moaned the heron. "Separate caucuses effective immediately. I will be by to see each of you."

Each group turned inward to form a huddle, from which a flat, indecipherable buzz emanated. The heron exhaled as it peered over at each of them, one of the kestrels gesturing wildly with its wings while the vultures bobbed their heads rhythmically. The heron looked up at the cloudy sky, hoping there would not be rain during its flight home.

"I deserve the largest part of the rat!" yelled the largest kestrel to its compatriots. "I have the largest appetite."

"I sunk my talons into it," answered one of the others. It grabbed a nearby twig with its foot, "just like that."

"Oh, please," said the third kestrel. "I was the one who spotted it. Had it not been for me, neither of you would have known it existed."

The vultures were no better. One stuck out its tongue, leading to an unceremonious smack upside the head from another's wing.

"What'd you do that for?"

"We are trying to secure a gigantic rat and you have devolved to boorish immaturity."

"I am not the one smacking people with my wing. I will have you know that is completely inappropriate."

"Maybe if we had smacked the kestrels a few times, we would have the rat by now," said the third vulture balefully. "The kestrels may well have killed the thing. For us to come away with it will take an outstanding effort."

The kestrels were similarly worried. "I dare say," noted the kestrel that had spotted the rat initially, "that the vultures' right may exceed ours. We killed the rat in their territory with them very close by. An inspection of the rat could yield that the wretch died of shock, and if it does, I do not know how we can legitimately claim a creature that did not die by our foot."

The heron passed between the groups, hearing what each had to say. Each admitted its respective predicament while also reiterating its central arguments. Neither side desired an inspection of the rat, as an unfavourable ruling would be devastating. Neither side would accept even the richest recompense for the prize. The heron saw no other simple solution.

The exhausted heron sat, eyes half closed, as the joint session reconvened.

HOW-TO: Run Off A Well-Intentioned, Handsome Man

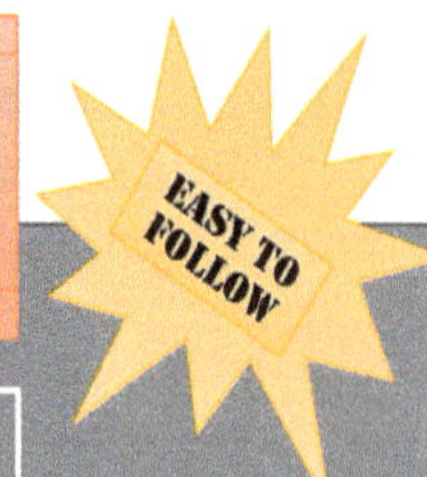

Erica Susan Saffer

A QUICK REFERENCE GUIDE FOR BEGINNERS

OPEN THE DATING DATABASE
First, attract well-intentioned, handsome man via attractionary methods below; apply liberally:
Broad Smile;
Adhere cosmetic embellishments;
Dramatize coquettish hair flip with follow up hair twirl.

ONCE INTEREST IS OBTAINED, generate conversation that revolves around:
Dining;
United acquisition of libations;
Interests leading to a proposal to collect around the consumption of aforementioned comforts, at an agreed upon time, at an agreed upon location.

ENGAGE NORMALIZED DATING PROTOCALS AND PROCEDURES

1-At time of meeting, guide conversation to include, but not be limited to:

a-shared interests, such as amateur taxidermy and underwear-clad backyard axe-throwing with a neighbor named Francois, who demands that you call him Francois, although the piece of mail that accidently came to your box names him specifically as Chuck Ryan Normous;

b-movies, such as the classics like the one movie, you know, with that actress, where they go to the store and get abducted? Reiterate how much you just love films;

c-art, like that funny print with the dog holding the pitchfork next to the cat wearing a lace collar against the background of a farmhouse, what's it called? *Veterinarian Gothic?* Reiterate how much you just love fine art;

d-music, especially local bands, which reminds you of;

SHARING PERSONAL HISTORY

2-The drummer from that one band you dated for 6 months, 7 months ago;

a-who had long black hair and hazel eyes, and licked his drumsticks before keeping time for his band, *The Enter-taint-ters;*

b-who once told you he "fucking loved you" only moments before vomiting Pabst Blue Ribbon and Fireball into your hair;

c-but you allowed him to move in anyway;

d-but not before you learned about the probation;

e-or how he attempts making ramen noodles at 4 am, blacked-out;

f-but instead burns down your kitchen and gets you evicted.

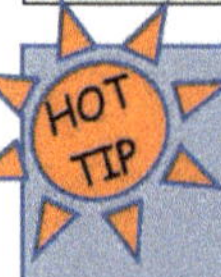

THEY SAY FIRST IMPRESSIONS ARE POWERFUL, BUT IF A PERSON STICKS AROUND AFTER MEETING YOU AT YOUR WORST, DON'T LET GO OF THEM, EVER. THEY'RE WORTH KEEPING.

CONTINUE
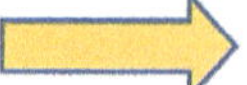

HELPFUL HINT: ***Perseverance is the essential key to any endeavor.***

3. Tell the well-intentioned, handsome man about the matching tattoos you and the drummer ex-boyfriend got at a kegger sitting side by side in matching folding chairs;
   - His: #GetYouSum;
   - Yours: #YOHO
     - (You-Only-Hoe-Once);
   - tell him how much you just love being a wordsmith.

4. Share your love of travel, although you've never left the state of Florida except for the time when you missed your exit to Yulee and had to turn around in St. Mary's and trek back across the Florida/Georgia line.

5. Forget how to annunciate vowels after slamming seven Long Island Iced Teas.

6. Begrudgingly accept the man's escort into the awaiting Uber he ordered you;

   a. but not without calling him a "Chad" first.

7. Attempt to kiss the well-intentioned, handsome man;

   a. dismiss his dismissal and fall into the backseat.

8. Send the man a message 10 seconds after the Uber departs, belittle him by fat-fingering "Little Whitney Bitch"

9. Complain to the Uber driver that the torn leather seats of his *Sloppy Jalopy* are hot;
   a. tell him you are snail-trailing down your inner thighs;
   b. demand he turn the air conditioning on max cool;
   c. ask him, "Did you hear me *Rico Slobby*?";
   d. make direct eye contact in the rear-view with a pair of awe-filled green eyes;

10. Lunge forward, grab the Uber driver's neck, which is also the neck of the drummer for the local band, *The Enter-taint-ters;*
    a. hold on tightly as the car careens into the ditch.

11. Call the handcuffing police officers *Stankzilla* and *Stankasaurus Rex;*
    a. make a pouty duckface mugshot;
    b. pass out; wake up; get released; charge phone; check social media;
    c. find out you have gone viral;
    d. proudly own the phrase #FloridaWoman.
    e. call well-intentioned, handsome man. Again. And again, and another 57 times in the next 33 minutes;
    f. answer the knock at the door;
    g. collect restraining orders from the delivery serviceman;
    h. laugh out loud.

But I've been showing restraint this whole time?

Like the time, last year, when insurance stopped paying for medication
and a $4.00 copay turned into a $273.00 full pay;

or the time the psychiatrist fell off the insurance plan,
so, you had to set appointments at a clinic 50 minutes and 63 days away;

when the fears returned to flex evil in your insomnia induced brain
and your unending days caused sights to form in shapes that scared you:

so, you called a high school friend and found a dealer who gave you little yellow bars of magic that quieted the voices;

but you had to stop those, too,

because *milk* and *gasoline* and *cheese wrapped in plastic cellophane* were more important;

and now, you think of; the police, the milk, the yellow bars, the cheese wrapped in plastic;

- **H**eaping it all into a gasoline-soaked pile;
- **E**ndeavoring to toss the lit match;
- **L**etting the flame burn off the screams of a life already on fire;
- **P**ausing for a moment, *showing restraint instead.*

River of Prose

Art by Jenn Conley
Poetry by Josephine Pino

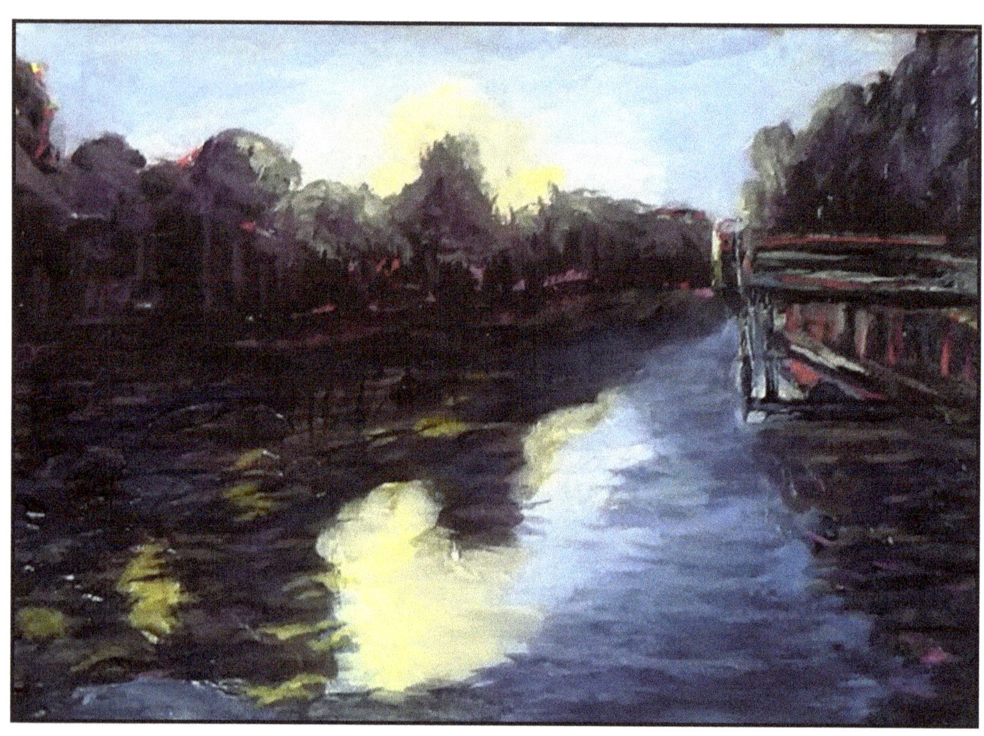

Shades of a bruise meander between mud-slick banks of joy and despair. The blush of filled capillaries glows eerie; the trappings of contentment are naught but mirrored ghosts, unlike the folds at the temple, the blurring of structured memories that seep, draining melancholy,

and still the opaque liquid keeps moving, cruising past pilings that hold slick algal thoughts too sessile to coalesce and thus they get caught in the stream and join the flow within veins, intrude into ganglia, and strive for direction, hopeful of a gushing spill or to be carried by paddles

one by one, lifted at first to the sky, then giving in to gravity and the downward pull, the turning of the wheel, the spillage and milling. And the words, unfettered like water molecules, dance. They revel amongst themselves, reflecting hues, revealing truths.

In Order Of Appearance:

Collin B. Randle lives in Irving, TX, with his wife and four children. He enjoys tending his 'fairytale' garden in his free time and is a writer as well.

Alexandra Hubbell holds BA in English Writing from NC State University, and is a locally produced playwright in her hometown of Raleigh, NC. She is known for several historical one-act plays produced by Burning Coal Theater Company, and for her Chrysalis Project award-winning three-act play, 'The Bridge'. She is currently working on her first novel and producing her first play out of Charleston, SC.

Cosper is an Oregon poet, painter and facilitator of creative experiments. Their self-published chapbook is entitled "Palm Sized Volcano." They have also authored and designed the creative-writing game "Sugar, Porridge, Spoons." They are the co-founder of Portland's "Winter Poetry Festival" and a graduate of the IPRC's Certificate Program in Poetry.

xiao yue shan is a poet and essayist born in china and residing in tokyo, japan. her website is shellyshan.com.

Ruben van Gogh (1967) is a Dutch poet and libretto writer, he has published 7 volumes of poetry and written over 10 opera librettos. Over the last 1,5 year he started to make smartphone-art: catchy images in which he combines several heavily altered photos, only using his smartphone and daily sceneries.

Juliet Lauren in an eighteen year old emerging writer. Her work can be found in Gold Wake Live, SkyIsland Journal, and Ghost City Review. Her manuscript and poetry have also been recognized numerous times by the Scholastic Arts and Writing Awards. She currently resides in Florida and you can follow her on instagram at jadore.mon.amour

Nadine Klassen is a 26 year-old emerging writer, born and currently living in Germany. Her work has appeared in Persephone´s Daughters third issue as well as Envision Art Show & Magazine and the Ink Spills Anthology by @Yourheartbeatsstrong. She otherwise publishes her work on social media using the name @emma.willows.writing.

Sophie Lee is from Seattle, Washington. Her work has been published by Bluefire, Canvas Teen Literary Journal, Prometheus Dreaming, and 4x4 Magazine. In her spare time, she does improv comedy, collages, and thinks about bees. She is currently a student at Columbia University.

Photographer Jada Fabrizio is passionately committed to story telling. She is an enthusiastic watcher of light and its effect it has on form. When she is not buliding sets in her studio or scuptling a creature for her photo stories she plays classical guitar and does freelance photography for medical institutions.Born in queens, New York, her formal education began at SUNY New Paltz. Where she studied creative writing and later photography at the School of Visual Arts And ICP (International Center of Photography) in New York City. Jada emphasizes the importance of capturing emotional experiences. "By not telling a complete story" she says, "It allows others to "feel" the photograph in their own way." She goes on to say, "I want the spectator to look at my photographs and experience their own reality through them."

Aminta Meheru writes poems everyday through linguistic experiments of erasure, selective conversation recording, and intentional manipulation of linguistic data. She also writes other ways. Her poem « Al » appears in Red Wheelbarrow Anthology (2017).

Florina Nastase is a teaching assistant at "Alexandru Ioan Cuza" University in Romania. She holds a PhD in American poetry, and spends too much time writing fan fiction online under various guises. She has been published in Kajet Journal and hopes to publish more original fiction.

Dave Sims was born in Pittsburgh, earned his MFA in Fairbanks, and spent over thirty years teaching writing and literature to thousands of diverse students in places ranging from the Arctic Slope to the bayous of Louisiana. Since emerging from the trenches of academe, he now dwells and creates in the mountains of central Pennsylvania. A multi-genre artist, his words and images appear on the covers and inside the pages of The Raw Art Review, Talking Writing, Freezeray, Burningword, The Nashville Review, Nunum and Arkana, with more comics and paintings forthcoming in Silver Needle, RiversEdge, and Stonecoast Review. He can be reached on Instagram at tincansims.

Mollie O'Leary received a B.A. from Kenyon College where she studied English and Philosophy. Her poems have been previously published or are forthcoming in HIKA Magazine, Riggwelter, and Cathexis Northwest Press. She grew up in Massachusetts and is currently an English teacher in Texas.

Ella Rous is a rising junior at the Westwood School in Dallas, Texas. She is preparing to enter the International Baccalaureate Diploma Program, and attended the Iowa Young Writer's Studio online course in poetry in 2018. Today, her favorite words are sepulchre, pearl, and tide.

Sasha Torchinsky is a queer artist born and raised in Vancouver, B.C. on the unceded traditional territory of the Musqueam, Squamish, and Tsleil-Waututh First Nations. Sasha is inspired by James Baldwin, reality television, and freaks everywhere. Sasha's photographic work explores and examines the intersectional nature of identity using Polaroid cameras modified for multiple film exposure.

Eros Livieratos studied philosophy and creative writing at William Paterson University. Eros' previous work can be found in The Esthetic Apostle, Cathexis Northwest Press, and Map Literary. Eros' writing tackles topics of race, sexuality, capitalism, aesthetics, and technology.

Sebastian Correa is a full-time student pursuing his MFA in fiction at Southern Connecticut State University. With fiction he like to delve into absurdism, surrealism, horror, magic realism, and satire that combines elements of philosophy, economics, and politics. Although a student of fiction, Sebastian also writes poetry, songs, and 'things' within the intersection of prose and verse.

Born in Los Angeles, by the age of seven she was handed a 110 camera and so began the journey into image-making Monica has studied studio art and art history in Europe and Asia and completed a "round the world trip" beginning in Nepal. Ms. Wiesblott currently exhibits her photography and printmaking both in the US and internationally. When she is not making art, you will find her planting flowers in her neighbor's yard or feeding the local birds. Monica currently lives in Southern California with her husband and spoiled cat.

Matthew Gordon's short fiction has appeared in Amazing Stories and on Smashwords. His non-fiction has appeared on RealGM, The Billfold, The Huffington Post and Sporting News. He is a member of the Toronto Writers' Cooperative, and is a writer and editor in Voices, its annual publication. He reviews a book each month at matthewgordonbooks.blogspot.com.

Erica Susan Saffer resides with her three children in Jacksonville, Florida, studied Education at Flagler College in Saint Augustine, Florida, and studies Fiction through the MFA Program at the University of Tampa. Her work provides rich and diverse insights into the beauty found in the mundane, as well as unearthing truths through voicing unique perspectives. She is currently writing a fiction novel, while planning a collection of short stories.

Jenn Conley is an acrylic artist from South Jersey. You can find more of her art on Facebook and Instagram. www.instagram.com/jenncbinspired/ www.facebook.com/JennConleyBInspired/

Josephine is an educator who continues to explore the ways that poetry, teaching and Biology not only play well together, they help each other thrive. She has published in El Portal, Cathexis NW, Curating Alexandria, and Raw Art Review, and featured in High Shelf and Tiny Seed Literary Journal.

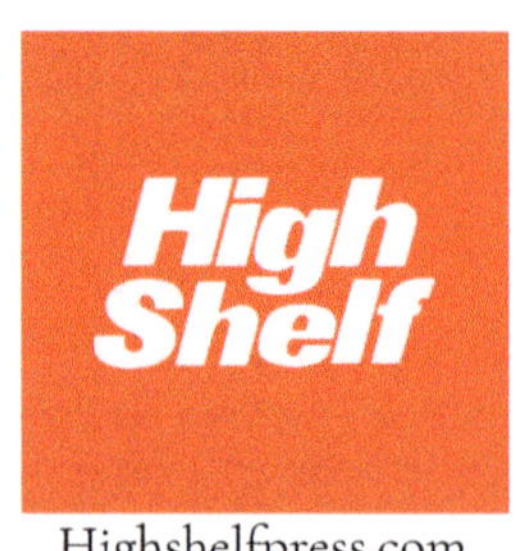

Highshelfpress.com

www.ingramcontent.com/pod-product-compliance
Ingram Content Group UK Ltd.
Pitfield, Milton Keynes, MK11 3LW, UK
UKHW062313290726
14090UKWH00018B/1049